Adobe

Adobe

Illustrator CS

CREATIVE STUDIO

Techniques for Digital Artists

Luanne Seymour Cohen

Adobe Illustrator CS Creative Studio, Techniques for Digital Artists
by Luanne Seymour Cohen

Copyright © 2004 by Luanne Seymour Cohen

This Adobe Press book is published by Peachpit Press.

For information on Adobe Press books, contact:
Peachpit Press
1249 Eighth Street
Berkeley, CA 94710
510/524-2178 (tel) / 510/524-2221 (fax)
To report errors, please send a note to errata@peachpit.com
Peachpit Press is a division of Pearson Education
For the latest on Adobe Press books, go to http://www.adobe.com/adobepress

Editor: Becky Morgan
Production Coordinator: Lisa Brazieal
Copyeditor: Judy Walthers von Alten
Book design/production: Jan Martí, Command Z
Cover design: Aren Howell

ISBN 0-321-22044-7

9 8 7 6 5 4 3 2 1

Printed and bound in the United States of America

Acknowledgments

It's the friends you can call up at 4 a.m. that matter.
—Marlene Dietrich

Creating a book like this is a very big project. There are hundreds of illustrations to do, thousands of words to write, rewrite, and edit. It takes many, many hours, weeks, days, and months. To write a book like this one is a full-time job. Being a glutton for punishment, I tried to write this book and go to graduate school at the same time. Silly me. After a couple of weeks of classes and homework, I started to panic. My friends and family pitched in and helped me, and I could not have finished without them. I especially want to thank two people who have helped me tremendously. Mordy Golding helped me write 10 of the techniques—in record time. He was, as always, good-natured, gracious, and very creative. My friend Leslie Cutler pitched in to help with all sorts of production chores. The day I found out that I had to redo all the illustrations at a different size, she offered her assistance and has been a godsend ever since. I literally could not have finished the book without these very dear friends. My book team, Judy Walthers von Alten, Jan Martí, Becky Morgan, and Lisa Brazieal have all stretched themselves to help me as well. Not only have they been great to work with, but they have been good friends and listeners as well. I thank you all from the bottom of my heart.

About the author

Luanne Seymour Cohen has been a graphic designer for the last 27 years. Some of the Silicon Valley companies she has worked for include Atari, Apple Computer, and Adobe Systems. She was a Creative Director at Adobe for 12 years where she created package designs and illustrations, and produced a variety of collateral materials for Adobe and its software products. She also developed and designed the Adobe Collector's Edition products. Her responsibilities included working closely with the engineers as an advisor during the development of Adobe's graphic software. She wrote and illustrated four editions of *Design Essentials* and another book in the series, *Imaging Essentials*. She has also written several books in the Adobe Press *Classroom in a Book* series. Her most recent book is *Adobe Photoshop CS Creative Studio*.

Some of her award-winning work has been shown in *Communication Arts*, *Print* magazine, the *Type Directors Club*, *Print* casebooks, and the AIGA annual. She has taught workshops and classes all over the world, including at Stanford University, Kent State University, University of California at Santa Barbara, Anderson Ranch Arts Center, Center for Creative Imaging, the Thunder Lizard Photoshop and Illustrator conferences, and California College of Arts and Crafts. An avid quilter for many years, she has taught classes and written articles on digital quilt and fabric design. Under her father's imprint in 1995, she published a book, *Quilt Design Masters* (Dale Seymour Publications/Addison Wesley), that is used in elementary school classrooms to teach mathematical principles. She lives and teaches in the San Francisco Bay Area.

Contents

Introduction

Adobe Illustrator CS Creative Studio shows how to produce traditional graphic and photographic effects using Adobe Illustrator CS software. This book does not attempt to describe all the features of the software program. Instead it is a quick, how-to recipe book for artists familiar with the basic tools and commands in the programs.

Each technique has been tested by professional designers, Web page designers, illustrators, teachers, photographers, and novice users. Although I assume that the reader has a basic working knowledge of the software, I have included an appendix that reviews the basic shortcuts and commands that I use every day with these programs. Most of the pages include tips and shortcut sidebars. Some are general tips that can be used with any technique. Some are specific additions or variations of the technique on that page.

Adobe Illustrator CS Creative Studio covers the most recent version of the software for both Macintosh and Windows platforms: Adobe Illustrator CS and Adobe Photoshop CS. Many, but not all, of these techniques can be used with older versions of the software. Look for the platform-specific shortcuts in the appendix. When keys are indicated in the text, I use a slash (/) to separate the Macintosh and Windows key needed. For example:

"Press Option/Alt when clicking a button" means

Mac OS X users press the Option key.

Windows users press the Alt key.

Unless mentioned otherwise, all files used in these techniques are in CMYK color mode.

Working efficiently

Deleting swatches and brushes quickly

Removing unused brushes, swatches, symbols, graphic styles, graph designs, and actions can reduce your file sizes considerably. If this is important, you can delete these items from their corresponding palettes fairly quickly. Here's how:

1 Open the palette that contains the items you want to delete.

2 To delete a group of items, click the first item in the palette list. Then Shift-click the last item to select it and all those listed between it and the first item.

3 To delete selected items all at once without displaying the warning dialog for each item, Option/Alt-click the Trash button at the bottom of the palette.

This book is full of tips and shortcuts to make working with Illustrator quicker and easier. Before you dive into the techniques, here are some basic tips on how to work more efficiently while using Illustrator. This is by no means an exhaustive guide on how to use each feature mentioned. For more information on the features or tools discussed here, see the Illustrator CS user guide or Illustrator Help.

Using templates to speed up your work

If you work on different types of projects, it can save you a lot of time if you set up a template for those jobs. For example, a different template was created for each of the different sizes of illustrations used in this book. One of the nice things about templates is that you can create as many of them as you want and save them anywhere on your hard drive. (This is not the case with startup files.) To create a template do the following:

1 Open a new or existing document.

2 Customize the document in any one of these ways:

• Set up the document window the way you want it to appear each time you create a new file with the template. Be sure to set the magnification level, scroll position, ruler origin, and options in the View menu.

• Create any artwork or guides that you want to appear in new documents you create from the template.

• Delete any existing swatches, styles, brushes, symbols, or actions that you don't want to keep. Deleting these can significantly reduce your file size.

- Create any new swatches, styles, brushes, symbols, and actions you want in the corresponding palettes.

- Set the options in the Document Setup dialog box and Print Options dialog box.

3 Choose File > Save As Template. Select a location for the file, enter a filename, and click Save. Illustrator will save the file in AIT (Adobe Illustrator Template) format.

To use the template, choose File > New from Template.

Using keyboard shortcuts

Use the keyboard to quickly change tools—Each tool in the toolbox has a letter shortcut assigned to it: just type the letter and the tool changes. To view the shortcuts, position the pointer over a tool in the toolbox. When the tooltip appears, the shortcut letter will appear next to the tool name. You can also find the tool shortcuts in Illustrator Help.

Use the keyboard to access menu items—Many of the menu commands have keyboard shortcuts. To view the shortcuts, choose a menu. The shortcut is displayed to the right of the command name. For a list of many of the shortcuts, see "Appendix A: Shortcuts" on page 312 or see Illustrator Help.

Customizing your keyboard shortcuts

If you are accustomed to using particular keyboard shortcuts with other programs or with older versions of Illustrator, you can customize the shortcuts. For example, to change the shortcut for a tool, choose Edit > Keyboard Shortcuts. Select the tool for which you want to change the shortcut. Click the Shortcut column for that tool and enter the new shortcut. The set name will change to Custom. Click OK. At the prompt, name the key set and click OK to save the set and apply the new set of shortcuts.

Measuring paths accurately

If you want the sizes in your Info, Align, and Transform palettes to recognize the size of the path instead of the size of a path with its stroke width added, turn off the Preview Bounds option.

When this option is on, Illustrator adds the stroke width that extends outside the path to the size of a path. For example, if you create a square that measures 100 points on each side and stroke it with an 8-point stroke, the Info palette will describe that square as 108 points square. That is because 4 points of the stroke extend beyond each of the four sides.

To change the setting, choose Command/Ctrl+K to open the Preferences dialog box. Toggle the setting on or off and click OK.

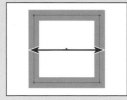

Preview Bounds on: square is measured from edge of stroke

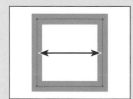

Preview Bounds off: square is measured from edge of path

To export a set of shortcuts to a text file, choose Edit > Keyboard Shortcuts, select a set, and click Export Text. In the Save Key Set File As dialog box, name the key set, and click Save. You can print out this file for a paper copy of your keyboard shortcuts.

Using presets

If you have certain settings that you use repeatedly, create presets for them. For example, illustrations for this book were printed on different printers. To save time, print presets were created for each draft, high-quality color, and thumbnail version. When it was time to print, the appropriate print preset was selected from the Print Preset pop-up menu in the Print dialog box.

To create a print preset, choose File > Print. Enter all the print settings and click Save Preset. Name the preset. It will appear in your Print Preset menu.

Using actions for repeated tasks

Use actions in the Actions palette—Choose an action from the action sets in the Actions palette.

Make your own actions—Make an action by recording a series of commands that you use frequently. For instructions on how to record an action, see the Illustrator CS user guide or Illustrator Help.

Use scripting to speed things up—Automate tasks with scripting. Illustrator supports Visual Basic scripting, AppleScript, and JavaScript. There are a few preset scripts that you can find by choosing File > Scripts > and then choosing the script you want from the menu. You can also write your own scripts. For more information, see the Illustrator Scripting Guide.pdf file on your Illustrator CS CD.

Using the Align palette for quick placement

Align to the artboard—To quickly align selected objects on the page, turn on the Align to Artboard option in the Align palette menu. Clicking the different Align Objects buttons in the Align palette aligns objects to the artboard's top, bottom, or center, depending on the selected option. Selecting the Use Preview Bounds option (see the tip at the left) aligns the stroked objects by their stroke edges, not the path edges.

Line up fast with Align palette—When you want to quickly align objects in relation to each other and not the artboard, turn off the Align to Artboard option by selecting it in the Align palette menu. Then select the objects, and click the Align Objects and Distribute Objects buttons until the objects are distributed as you like.

Creating views for easy zooming

When you are creating a complex illustration, you can create several views of the illustration to make it easier to edit. Some illustrations can take a long time to redraw when you are constantly zooming in and out to edit, especially when you use 3D effects and other graphic styles. Say, for example, you are creating a drawing of a complex 3D object and you want to zoom in to work on a small detail. You can create a view of the zoomed in area of detail. Then you can create another view of the object as a whole so that you can quickly pop back and forth between views as you edit.

To create a new view, set up the view and zoom level first. Then choose View > New View. Name the view and click OK. Repeat this procedure for each view you want to create. When you want to access the view, choose View and select the name of your view at the bottom of the View menu.

Simplifying complex paths

Sometimes paths can get very complex and are difficult or impossible for some printers to print. If you are having trouble printing, it could be because the paths are too complex and the printer's memory is overloaded. Try simplifying some of the complex paths by doing this:

1　Select the path.
2　Choose Object > Path > Simplify.
3　Turn on the Preview option and adjust the settings until the path is simpler and the preview is satisfactory.
4　Click OK to apply the filter.

Original artwork: 279 points

Simplify Path		
Curve Precision	95	%
Angle Threshold	0	°
Original: 279 pts	Current: 72 pts	

Apply Simplify Path to reduce points

Final artwork: 72 points

Section 1 Painting

1 Scribble painting

Flamenco
in the Park

Friday evenings
6pm to 9pm
Cuesta Park Gazebo

Use the Scribble effect for some interesting line textures, especially when adding multiple layers of scribbling for a cross-hatch effect. For a painterly effect, use the Scribble effect and then expand and paint the resulting strokes with a paintbrush. Try varying the paintbrushes and their sizes for different effects.

1   Create a shape that you want to be scribble-painted. Paint the shape with a colored fill and a stroke of None.

Create a filled shape

2   With the shape still selected, choose Effect > Stylize > Scribble. Turn on the Preview option. Use the settings in the following illustration or create your own custom settings to make a loose, loopy scribble. The scribble should overlap the edges of the shape in some areas. When you are satisfied with the effect, click OK.

Apply the Scribble effect

Scribble effect applied to shape

3 Choose Object > Expand Appearance to convert the scribbles into simple strokes.

Expand the appearance

4 Select the scissors tool in the toolbox. Cut up the paths
that the Scribble effect created by clicking once on the spot
where you want the cut. Try to cut the paths on the outside
curves.

Often the Scribble effect creates a few very long paths. You
will add brushstrokes to the paths in a later step; cutting the
paths now will improve the painting's looks. In the following
example, the scribbled shape started with just 2 paths. After
cutting, the shape consisted of 15 paths.

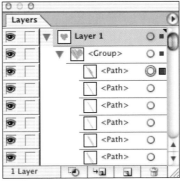

Scribbled shape before cutting   *Scribbled shape after cutting*

Select groups and paths quickly

It is sometimes easier to select grouped items or parts of groups by using the Layers palette. To select a group, click the area to the right of the target circle and the group name. To select just a path, click the area to the right of the target circle and the path name. To add to the selection, Shift-click the area to the right of the target circle of another path name.

Click to the right of the target circle to select

Group and its paths selected

5 Choose Window > Brushes to display the Brushes palette.

6 Open the Artistic_Ink brush library by choosing Open Brush Library from the Brushes palette menu and choosing Artistic_Ink library from the pop-up menu.

7 Select all the paths in the scribbled shape. Either use the selection tool or click to the right of the target circle in the Layers palette next to the <Group> item that represents the scribbled shape.

8 With the scribbled group selected, click the Light Ink Wash brush in the Brushes palette to apply it to the strokes. (To display the brushes by name, choose List View from the palette menu.)

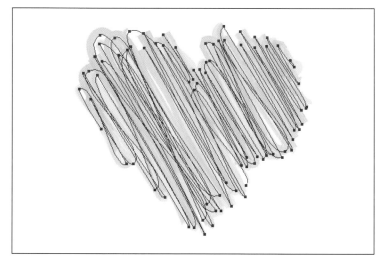

Paint the strokes with the Light Ink Wash brush

9 If you want to see the effect better, choose View > Hide Edges (Command/Ctrl+H) to hide the selection. Try different brushes for different effects.

10 To change the color of the brush stroke, use the Color palette to select another stroke color. Even though it may look like a filled shape, brushes take their color from the stroke of the selected path, not the fill.

11 If you hid the selection edges in step 9, redisplay them by choosing View > Show Edges. Deselect.

Completed Scribbled painting

Variation: Different color fill

For an interesting color variation, in step 10 when changing the stroke color, add a fill that differs from the stroke color.

Add a different color fill

2 | Neon graphics and type

Making graphics glow in Illustrator is easy, but making digital neon is a different matter. Real neon signs and graphics are made from colored tubes filled with gas. The tubes are the same width and are wrapped and twisted to make shapes and letterforms. To make digital neon, use paths and then create a tubal gradation by layering progressively smaller stroked paths on top of each other in the Appearance palette. This method is very versatile because you can save the appearance as a style, edit it, and reuse it without re-creating the neon each time.

Digital neon

1 Create a Background layer that is black or contains very dark tones to set off the neon artwork. Lock the Background layer. Make a new layer and name it Neon.

2 On the Neon layer, create the neon artwork using the pen tool or a shape creation tool (for example, star, rectangle, and so on). Leave plenty of space between the paths so that you can increase the line thickness.

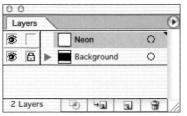

Create a black Background layer

Targeting vs. selecting

To target a layer, click the circle to the right of the layer name in the Layers palette. Targeting a layer means that anything you do, such as add an effect or change the transparency, will affect everything on that layer. Also, if you add another object after you've targeted the layer and added an effect, that object will adopt the effect as well.

If you click to the right of the circle, you will select everything on that layer. You can alter the selected objects by adding effects or changing the appearance. But if you add another object to that layer later on, it will not be affected by the changes.

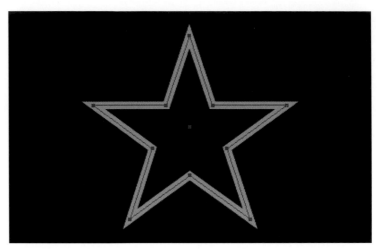

Create the neon artwork

3   Choose Show Options from the Stroke palette menu. Select the Round Cap and Round Join options.

These options make the stroked paths look more like curved tubes.

4   With the path or paths still selected, choose a fill of None and a stroke of None.

The neon paint colors will be added as an appearance for the Neon layer. If individual paths are already painted, their paint can change or obscure the look of the neon style.

5   In the Layers palette, click the target indicator for the Neon layer. Targeting a layer lets you affect the entire layer when you add an appearance.

Select round endcaps and joins   *Target the Neon layer*

6   From the Appearance palette menu, choose Add New
    Stroke.

A stroke is added with the default color and width. You will
change these in the next steps.

7   Select the stroke weight and choose the Round Cap and
    Round Join options. This stroke will be the base color and
    the widest stroke of the neon tube.

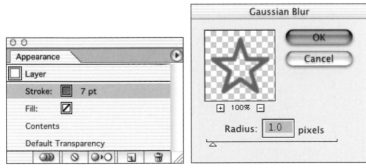

Choose Add New Stroke   *Change the stroke weight, cap, and join*

8   In the Color palette, change the stroke color to the base
    color of the neon. This will be the darkest part of the neon
    tube.

9   With the stroke still selected in the Appearance palette,
    choose Effect > Blur > Gaussian Blur. Set the radius and
    click OK.

Change the stroke color   *Add a Gaussian Blur effect*

10 Evaluate the base level of the neon. If the Gaussian Blur
    effect appears too blurred or jagged, you may want to

change the effect's resolution. The default resolution is 72 ppi. If you want to change it, continue with step 11. If not, go to step 12.

11 To change the raster settings for the Gaussian Blur effect, choose Effect > Document Raster Effects Settings. Select the resolution desired and click OK.

The higher the resolution, the longer it will take for your graphics to preview.

Evaluate the base layer

Adjust the raster settings

12 Make sure that the Neon layer is still targeted. Select the stroke in the Appearance palette, and choose Duplicate Item from the palette menu.

13 Reduce the stroke weight and change the color to a lighter version of the base color. Double-click the Gaussian Blur item to reopen the Gaussian Blur dialog box. Reduce the amount of blur.

In this example, the Gaussian Blur amount was reduced by half to match the stroke weight reduced by nearly half.

Appearance ▶	Appearance ▶
☐ Layer	☐ Layer
▼ Stroke:	▼ Stroke:
Color: ■ 7 pt	Color: ■ 4 pt
Gaussian Blur	Gaussian Blur
▼ Stroke:	▼ Stroke:
Color: ■ 7 pt	Color: ■ 7 pt
Gaussian Blur	Gaussian Blur
Fill: ☑	Fill: ☑
Contents	Contents
Default Transparency	Default Transparency

Duplicate the stroke   *Adjust the weight, color, and blur*

14 Repeat steps 12 and 13 to create one last stroke. This one will represent the brightest, hottest part of the neon effect. Make the color bright and much lighter than the other two. Reduce the stroke weight and Gaussian blur as well.

Evaluating effects and their resolution

Changing the resolution in the Document Raster Effects Settings dialog box may change how the effects look. For example, a Gaussian blur of 1.0 pixels looks very pronounced at Screen resolution (72 ppi), but it is barely noticeable at High resolution (300 ppi). Once you've changed your document resolution, go back and check all the effects and appearances. You may need to adjust some of them to accommodate the new resolution.

15 Evaluate the effect. Depending on the resolution you chose in step 11, the stroke weight and blur amount will vary. The higher the resolution, the higher the blur amount will need to be for a smooth, rounded effect. If you need to adjust colors, stroke weights, or blur amounts, just double-click them in the Appearance palette and change the values.

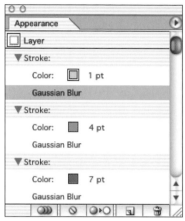

Create the brightest part of the neon

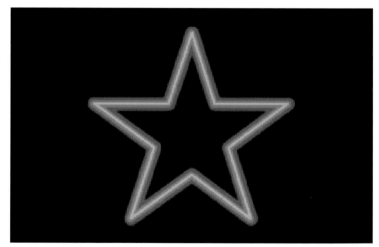

Evaluate the effect

Neon effect as a graphic style

1   Position the Appearance palette and the Graphic Styles palette so that they are both visible. Drag the thumbnail of the appearance from the Appearance palette onto the Graphic Styles palette until a thick, black border appears. Release the mouse button to create a style. If you want to name it, double-click the thumbnail in the Graphic Styles palette and enter a name.

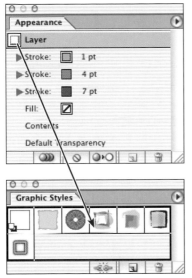

Save the appearance as a graphic style

2   Apply the style you created to layers or individual paths. You can also change the style's colors or stroke weights to create a new style.

Adding strokes in the Appearance palette

Why add strokes in the Appearance palette instead of just copying a stroke and pasting it on top of the original? There are a couple of good reasons. First, it's easier to select the different strokes in the Appearance palette. When you have several versions of the same path stacked on top of each other, selecting can become difficult. Second, once you've created the multiline appearance, you can save it as a graphic style and use it over again on other shapes, layers, or files.

In this example, the neon style was applied to the rectangle and then the colors for each stroke were changed. The resolution was set to Medium (150 ppi).

Original and revised graphic style applied to artwork

Making neon type

Creating neon type is a little different than creating a neon graphic. You need to decide if you want the type to be the thickness of one neon "tube" or if you want the typeface to be outlined with a neon tube.

If you want the typeface to be outlined, just follow the directions for neon graphics. Be sure to choose a typeface that is large and bold so that the outlines don't touch as they go around the letterforms. Sans-serif typefaces tend to work best for this purpose.

If you want to create neon type that is the thickness of one tube, use an existing typeface as a guide and then create paths that mimic it. You might be thinking, why not just outline the typeface? When you convert typefaces to outlines, they become closed shapes. What you need here is unclosed paths that can be stroked with the neon graphic style.

1 Select a thin or light typeface and type the word or words that you want to create in neon.
2 Fill the typeface with 20% black.
3 Choose Object > Lock > Selection to lock the type. It will now be used as a template for tracing.
4 Select the pen tool and set the paint values to no fill and a black stroke of 1 point.
5 Trace the letterforms carefully with the pen tool. Make a new path for each letter.

Paint type with 20% black

Trace letterforms with the pen tool

6 Follow the instructions in "Neon effect as a graphic style" on page 21 for making a neon graphic style.
7 Select the type paths and apply the neon graphic style to them.

Single "tube" neon type

Outlined neon type using typeface

3 | Simple patterns

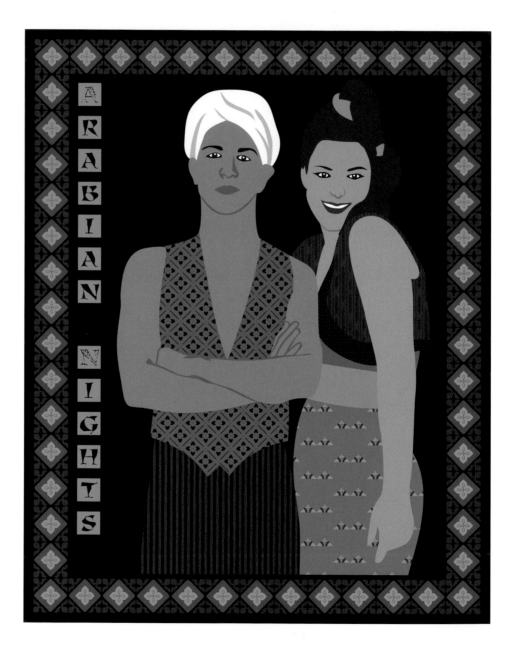

The simplest way to construct a pattern tile is to draw any graphic object and surround it with a rectangle placed in the background. This procedure describes how to take it a step further: You can create dense patterns that tile perfectly by positioning copies of the graphic in each corner of the background rectangle. Once you've created the basic pattern tile, you can transform it with any of the transformation tools. You can also make copies of the tile and create different color variations for dcsign experimentation.

1   Select the rectangle tool and create a rectangle that's the desired size of your pattern tile. For the most efficient printing and previewing, try to keep it between 1 and 2 inches square.

Note: Do not use the rounded rectangle tool for this step. The rectangle must have square corners.

2   Fill the rectangle with the background color of your pattern. If you want the pattern to have a transparent background, fill and stroke it with None. If you want a solid background, stroke it with None.

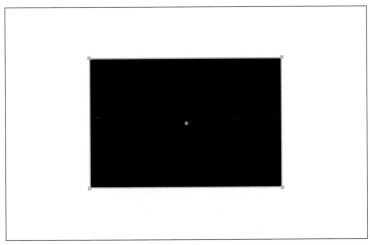

Create the background rectangle

3   Create or copy and paste the artwork that you want to use as a repeating element in your pattern. Check the View

menu to make sure that the Snap to Point and Smart Guides options are turned on.

4   Skip this step if the element is the correct size for the pattern. If the element needs to be scaled, select the scale tool in the toolbox and scale the element.

The element must be small enough that copies can fit in the center and in each of the four corners without touching each other.

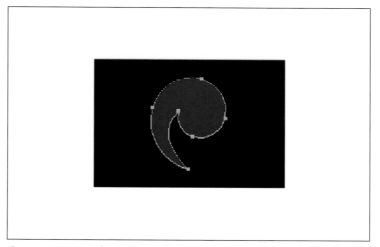

Create a repeating element

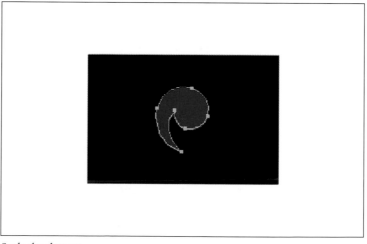

Scale the element

5 Choose Window > Attributes to display the Attributes palette. With the object selected, click the Show Center button to display the center point of the element.

6 Use the selection tool and grab the element by the center point. Drag it until it snaps to the upper left corner point of the rectangle. Don't release the mouse button until the pointer becomes a white arrowhead, indicating that the points have snapped.

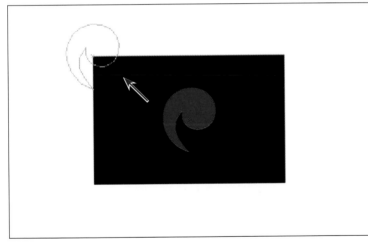

Display the center point

Drag the element to the upper left corner

7 Grab the element again by its center point. Begin to drag it, and then press Shift and Option/Alt to constrain and copy it. Drag until it snaps to the upper right corner point of the rectangle. Don't release the mouse button until the cursor

What can't be in a pattern?

- Patterns
- Gradients
- Raster images
- Embedded art and images
- Mesh objects
- Brush strokes
- Blends
- Symbol instances
- Effects
- Graphs
- Masks

If you want to use the artwork from any of the above items in a pattern, select the artwork and choose Object > Expand. With the exception of placed images, the artwork should be useable in a pattern tile after applying the Expand command.

Shortcut: Paste objects front or back

Instead of copying and pasting objects in front or in back of other objects, try using the Layers palette. Select the object. In the Layers palette, that selection will show up as a blue dot to the right of the layer name. Click the triangle next to the layer name to expand it and to reveal the artwork on that layer. Now press Option/Alt, click the blue dot and drag down to place a copy of the object behind the original. Drag up to place a copy of the object in front of the original. Release the mouse and then Option/Alt.

becomes a white arrowhead, and the intersect hint appears. Release the mouse button and then Shift and Option/Alt.

8   Select both top elements. Grab the right element by its center point. Begin to drag it down, and then press Shift and Option/Alt. Drag until it snaps to the lower right corner point of the rectangle. Release the mouse button and then Shift and Option/Alt.

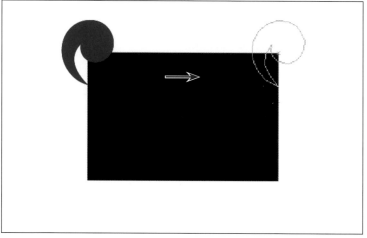

Slide the copy to the right corner

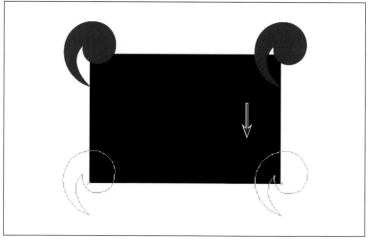

Slide the copies to the lower corners

9 Place any additional graphics you want within the rectangle. Make sure that these elements don't overlap the rectangle edges. If they do, the pattern won't tile correctly.

In the example below, a rotated version of the element was added and its center point was placed over the center point of the rectangle.

10 If you are already using a transparent rectangle as a background, skip to step 12. If your rectangle is stroked or filled, select the rectangle. Choose Edit > Copy and, while the rectangle is still selected, choose Edit > Paste in Back. Do not deselect yet.

It won't look like it, but you now have two rectangles stacked on top of each other.

11 With the backmost rectangle still selected, paint it with a stroke and fill of None.

This invisible rectangle will become the bounding box for the pattern tile. It defines the edges of the tile.

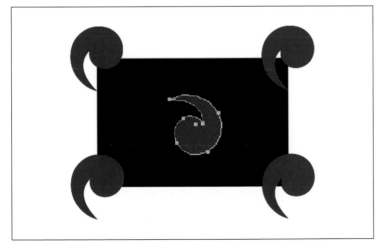

Place the center element

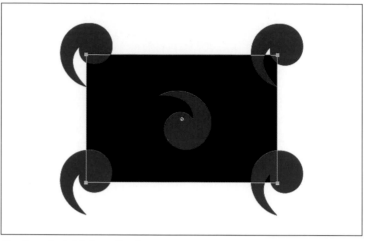

Create an invisible bounding box

12 Choose the selection tool in the toolbox and marquee-select both the rectangles and all of the pattern elements.

13 Choose Edit > Define Pattern. Name your pattern and click OK. The new pattern tile will appear in the Swatches palette.

14 Create a shape, and then click the tile you just created in the Swatches palette to fill the shape with your new pattern.

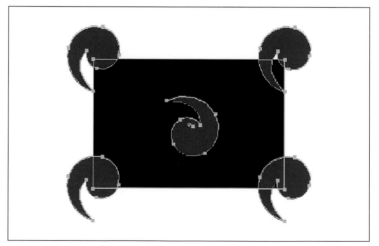

Select all objects and define a pattern

Test the pattern within a large shape

Transforming a pattern within a shape

If you want to transform a pattern within a shape while leaving the shape intact, use one of the following methods. To transform precisely:

1. Select the object filled with a pattern.
2. Double-click the transformation tool in the toolbox.
3. In the Options section of the dialog box, select the Patterns option and deselect the Objects option. Then enter the amount you want to transform the pattern.
4. Click the Preview option; when you are satisfied with the result, click OK.

To transform by dragging:

1. Select the object filled with a pattern.
2. Select a transformation tool in the toolbox.
3. Hold down the ~ (tilde) key and drag the transformation tool to transform the pattern. Release the mouse button to view the result.

This method is quicker than using a dialog box but less accurate.

4 | Texture patterns

You can create the effect of an uneven texture by constructing a pattern that appears irregular when it tiles. To achieve this effect, the edges of the pattern tile must match perfectly so that the tiling creates one continuous texture. These textures take time to finesse; once you've got a tile that works, try making different versions of it with different colors and stroke weights. If you need something quick, start with some premade tiles by loading the Pattern Samples libraries that came with your program. Then customize the tile for your own needs.

1 Use the rectangle tool to create a rectangle the size you want your pattern tile to be.

For the most efficient printing and previewing, try to keep the rectangle between 1 and 2 inches square.

Note: Do not use the rounded rectangle tool for this step. The rectangle must have square corners.

2 Fill the square with the background color of your pattern. If you want the pattern to have a transparent background, fill and stroke it with None. Begin drawing the texture with just the shapes or lines that intersect the left side of the square. Select the square and the texture.

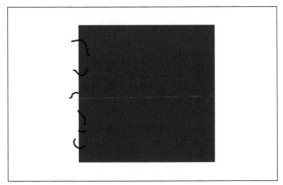

Add texture that intersects the left edge

Transforming patterns and their fills

If you always want your pattern tiles to transform along with the objects they fill, choose Illustrator > Preferences > General (Mac OS X) or Edit > Preferences > General (Windows) and select the Transform Pattern Tiles option.

3   Check the View menu to make sure that the Snap to Point and Smart Guides options are turned on. Position the pointer on the lower left corner of the square. Begin dragging the artwork to the right; then press Shift and Option/Alt to constrain the move and leave a copy. When the cursor snaps to the lower right corner point, release the mouse button and then Shift and Option/Alt.

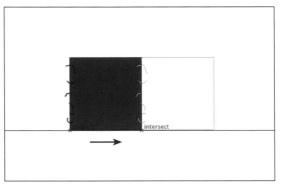

Slide a copy of the texture and rectangle to the right edge

4   Select the right square and delete it.

5   Continue drawing your texture by adding shapes or lines that intersect only the top of the square. When you have finished, select the rectangle and the top texture only.

Delete the right square

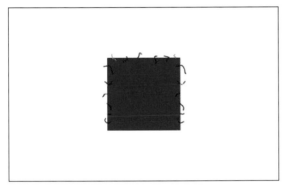

Add texture to the top edge

6 Position the pointer on the upper right corner of the
square. Begin dragging the artwork down; then press Shift
and Option/Alt to constrain the move and leave a copy.
When the cursor snaps to the lower right corner point,
release the mouse button and then Shift and Option/Alt.

7 Select the lower square and delete it.

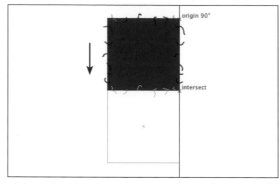

Slide a copy of the texture and rectangle to the bottom edge

Delete the bottom square

8   Fill in the middle of the square with your texture. Be careful not to intersect any of the square's edges or corners.

9   For a more varied texture, use more than one color for the texture elements. If you repaint any edge pieces, be sure to paint the corresponding edge piece on the opposite side the same way.

Subtle color differences enhance the illusion that this is a texture instead of a repeating pattern.

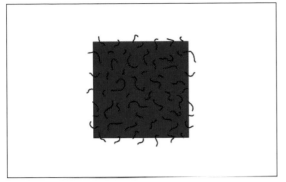

Fill the middle with texture

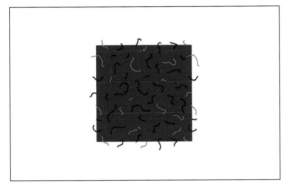

Add color if desired

How fill patterns tile

Fill patterns tile from left to right beginning at the 0,0 ruler origin. The ruler origin is determined by the rulers. The default is set to the bottom left corner of the page. To change the ruler origin, display the rulers by choosing View > Show Rulers. Then grab the cross hairs at the top left corner of the rulers and drag them into your document. Once the new ruler origin is where you want it, release the mouse button. Notice that all fill patterns within the file will change— even if they aren't selected.

10 If you are already using a transparent square as a background, skip to step 12. If your square is stroked or filled, select the square. Choose Edit > Copy and then Edit > Paste in Back. Do not deselect yet.

You now have two squares stacked on top of each other. One becomes a bounding box.

Overlapping patterns to make a complex texture

When you create a pattern tile with an invisible background, you can overlap it onto other shapes to create a texture over a large area or several shapes at once. A good example of this would be if you created a snowflake texture. You could create a whole scene and then make one large shape filled with the snowflake texture. Because the pattern background is invisible, you would see through it everywhere except where there were snowflakes.

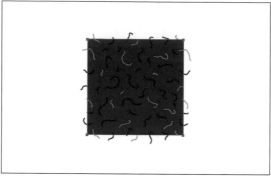

Create an invisible bounding box

11 With the backmost square still selected, paint it with a stroke and fill of None.

12 Select the squares and the texture elements. Choose Edit > Define Pattern. Name your pattern and click OK. The new pattern swatch will appear in the Swatches palette.

13 Create a large rectangle, and select the pattern in the Swatches palette to fill the rectangle with the new pattern. Zoom out and look for places in the texture that create an obvious repeating pattern. If necessary, return to the pattern tile and adjust the artwork to smooth out obvious holes or clumps. The goal is to get a smooth, even texture with no obvious repetition.

Variation: Inverted pattern texture

Once you've got a texture that works, create different color versions so that you can use the texture more than once.

1   Select the pattern tile from step 10.

2   Choose Filter > Colors > Invert Colors. Then continue with step 11 and complete the technique.

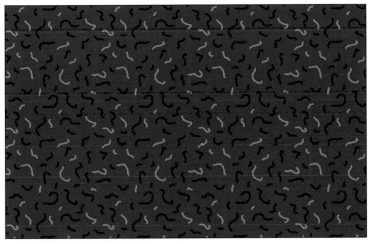

Test the pattern in a large shape

Create different color versions

5 Confetti paintings

Using a raster image, you can create tiles that can be overlapped for a tissue-paper or confetti collage look or that can be organized with "grout" for a mosaic effect. Start with an illustration or a placed raster image, and begin experimenting. Leave the original artwork on a layer in the background to fill in the holes that are left when transforming the tile artwork. You can also remove that layer for a confetti effect. For a stained glass effect, use black grout. Use images with big, bold shapes that are recognizable. Small details will be simplified and lost.

Confetti effect

1   Create or open an illustration. If the artwork exists on several layers, choose Flatten Artwork from the Layers palette menu to reduce the file to one layer.

If you are using a placed image, be sure to deselect the Link option when you place it. Because you are creating an impressionistic painting from the photograph, you may want to increase the saturation of the colors in the image before you place it in Illustrator.

If you want to retain the file with separate layers, choose File > Save As, and save the flattened file with a different name.

2   Drag the flattened layer onto the New Layer button at the bottom of the Layers palette to make a duplicate layer. Double-click the duplicate to open the Layer Options dialog box, and name the copy Confetti. Lock and hide the original layer.

3   Choose Select > All.

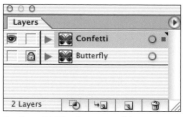

Lock and hide the original layer

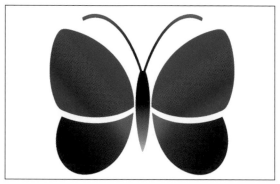

Select all

4   If you are using a placed image, skip to the next step. If you are using Illustrator artwork, choose Object > Rasterize to rasterize the selected image. Set the Anti-Aliasing option to Art Optimized (Supersampling). Select either Medium or Screen resolution. Click OK.

Because you will change this image to a mosaic of shapes, you don't need a high-resolution raster image.

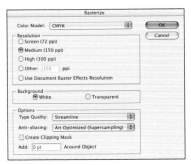

Rasterize the Illustrator artwork

5 With the selection still active, choose Filter > Create > Object Mosaic to turn the raster image into a mosaic of squares. Select the Delete Raster option, and enter the number of tiles you want for the Width. Click the Use Ratio button to have the height calculated and entered for you. Click OK.

6 Choose Object > Ungroup to release the mosaic tiles from their group. Choose View > Hide Edges so that the object remains selected and you can see the effect you will create in the next step.

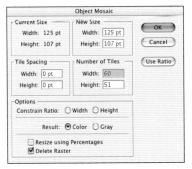

Convert the image to tiles

Transforming several shapes simultaneously

When you want to transform several shapes at once by the same amount, use the Transform Each command. Make sure that the selected shapes are not grouped with each other. Applying Transform Each to a group will transform the group as if it were one shape.

You can transform from the centers of each object or from another reference point. Click the point of reference locator to change the point. For example, to rotate several squares by their upper left corner, click the upper left point on the reference locator.

The Random option lets you transform objects by random amounts. For example, if you enter 30° for the rotation value and select the Random option, the objects will be rotated anywhere between 0° and 30°.

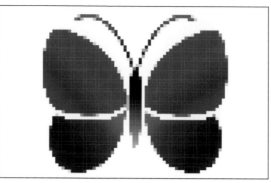

Ungroup the tiles and hide the edges

7   Choose Object > Transform > Transform Each to alter the tiles individually. Turn on the Preview option and increase the Scale values so that the tiles overlap. Turn on the Random option and change the Move and Rotate values for an irregular effect. When you are satisfied with the preview, click OK.

8   Choose View > Show Edges and then Select > Deselect to view the results.

If you are satisfied with the results, save your file. To try different background ideas, continue with the next step.

Transform the tiles

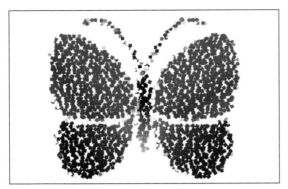

Deselect

Variation: Darkened confetti background

1 Lock the Confetti layer in the Layers palette and unlock and show the original layer.

2 Select different shapes on the original layer and alter their color slightly to set off the squares on the Confetti layer. Save the file.

In this example, the colors in the original gradients were darkened slightly.

Paint the original shapes with slightly darker colors

Shortcut: Lighten or darken a CMYK color

To quickly lighten or darken a CMYK color mix while keeping the color proportions, hold down Shift as you drag a slider in the Color palette. Dragging to the left lightens the color; dragging to the right darkens it. Once one of the colors equals 100% or 0%, you won't be able to change the color mix proportionately by Shift-dragging.

Removing white confetti

If you rasterized shapes that you created in Illustrator instead of using a placed image, you may find that your confetti image contains lots of white confetti. If you want to remove just the white shapes and leave the colored ones, follow these simple steps.

1 Unlock the Confetti layer and use the direct selection tool to select one of the white shapes. Check the Color palette to make sure that the shape is really painted white. Some of the shapes may be slightly tinted.

2 Choose Select > Same > Fill Color to select all the white shapes in the artwork.

3 Press Delete/Backspace to remove the shapes.

Variation: Solid or gradient confetti background

1 Lock the Confetti layer in the Layers palette and create a new layer in the Layers palette named Background.

2 Create a shape in the background and fill it with either a solid color or a gradient. Be sure to use colors that differ slightly from the colors in the confetti, to prevent the background shapes from disappearing.

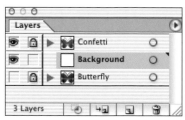

Create a new Background layer

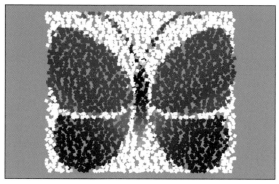

Create a background shape

Variation: Tissue-paper confetti

This effect works best if you are using a white background. Colored backgrounds will change the colors in the illustration because its transparency mode is set to Soft Light. If you want to put the illustration on a colored background, follow the instructions in "Creating tissue paper with a colored background" on page 48.

1   Follow the Confetti Effect technique, except in step 7 use larger Scale values.

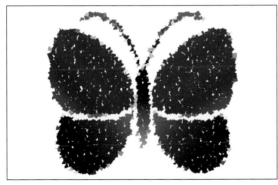

Use larger Scale values to create overlapping shapes

Overlapped tiles

2   With the tiles still selected, display the Transparency palette and choose the Soft Light blending mode.

Creating tissue paper with a colored background

If you want to place your tissue-paper collage on top of a colored background and control the color change, try these steps:

1 Follow step 1 of the Tissue-paper Confetti variation.

2 Target the Confetti layer in the Layers palette. Choose Effect > Pathfinder > Soft Mix. Use a 50% mix and click OK.

The effect is more subtle than when you use the Tissue-paper Confetti variation. But this technique has the advantage of letting you place a background underneath the collage image without changing the colors.

Note: The effect works only if you apply the blending mode to the selected tiles. If you apply the effect just to the layer, you won't see the overlapping transparent tiles.

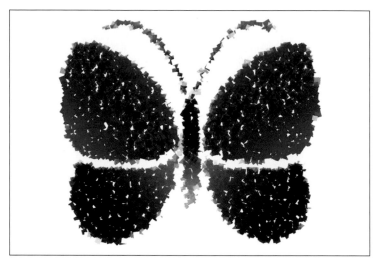

Overlapping transparent tiles

Variation: Mosaic tiles with grout

1 Follow steps 1 through 6 of the Confetti Effect technique. Create a new layer and name it Grout. Move it just below the Confetti layer. Create a rectangle the same size as the raster image rectangle, and fill it with a color that will appear between the tiles in the next step. Lock the Grout layer.

2 Continue with step 7 of the Confetti Effect technique, but reduce only the Horizontal and Vertical Scale percentages until the Grout layer appears through the Tissue Paper layer. For an even thickness of grout, use the same value for both Horizontal and Vertical Scale. Make sure that the values for Move and Rotate are set to 0. Click OK.

Create a grout layer   *Scale the tiles proportionally*

3   Save the file. Because the grout is on a separate layer, you
    can easily select it and try as many different colors as you
    like.

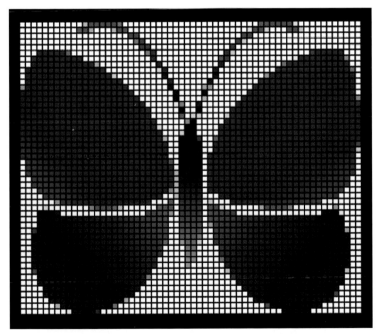

Mosaic tiles with grout

6 Colorized images

Colorized images are a necessity when designing art that will be printed in custom spot colors. Even for process-color artwork, monotone images can add a stylized look to any design. You'll start by placing a photograph in Illustrator. You can then explore the many ways to get the perfect look for your design.

You can place two kinds of raster images in Illustrator: A 1-bit black-and-white image (no shades of gray are supported), for a sharp-edged, not soft antialiased, effect; and an 8-bit grayscale or full-color image, which can be saved from Photoshop in just about any image format.

Both Place techniques work whether or not the Link option in the Place dialog box is selected. Unlinked placed images are embedded in the Illustrator file. Linked placed images can be edited in the application that created them and automatically updated in your Illustrator file via the Edit Original command.

Colorized 1-bit image

1   Choose File > Place to import a 1-bit TIFF image. You can use any image from Photoshop that has been converted to Bitmap mode and saved as a TIFF file. (Convert color images first to Grayscale and then Bitmap mode.)

Place a 1-bit TIFF image

Embedding images later

If you choose to link your image and then decide instead to embed the image, you don't have to place the photo again. Simply open the Links palette, select the linked file, and choose Embed Image from the palette menu.

2   Choose Window > Appearance. With the image selected, select the Fill item in the Appearance palette. In the Color palette, choose CMYK from the palette menu and then select a color in the color bar.

You can colorize 1-bit images with process and spot colors, but you cannot specify pattern or gradient fills. Any area of the bitmap image that was white in Photoshop will become transparent in Illustrator. If you want a white background, you can draw an additional white box behind the image.

Colorized 1-bit TIFF image

Colorized 8-bit image

1   Choose File > Place to import an 8-bit image into Illustrator. This technique works whether or not the Link option in the Place dialog is selected.

The method for colorizing 8-bit images in Illustrator is a bit more detailed than for a 1-bit image, but it offers more options.

Place an 8-bit image

Shortcut: Select stacked objects in the Layers palette

The Layers palette is a great place to select objects that are stacked directly on top of each other.

1 Display the Layers palette by choosing Window > Layers.
2 In the list, find the first path you want to select and click the area to the right of its target circle. A colored dot will appear to indicate that the path is selected.
3 Find the second path in the list and Shift-click the area to the right of its target circle to add the path to the selection.

2 With the image still selected, choose Window > Info to open the Info palette. Note the image's height and width for use in the next step.

3 Select the rectangle tool in the toolbox. Click once and enter the Height and Width values you noted in step 2. Move the rectangle to completely cover the placed image.

Info		
X : 2.3863 in	W : 3.7109 in	
Y : 6.7546 in	H : 2.5088 in	

Rectangle

Options
Width: 3.7109 in
Height: 2.5088 in

OK
Cancel

Note the width and height   *Create a rectangle*

4 Select a fill color for the rectangle that you just drew. The selected color will be applied to the image. You can choose process colors, spot colors, gradients, or patterns.

5 With just the rectangle selected, choose Object > Arrange > Send Backward. The rectangle must be directly beneath the image for this to work. You should now see the placed photograph on top of the colored rectangle. (You won't be able to see the rectangle.)

Painting an image with a gradient or pattern

For an interesting variation on the colorized image, try a gradient or pattern instead of a solid color. To create this effect, follow the Colorized 8-bit Image technique. In step 4, instead of filling the rectangle with a solid color, use a gradient or pattern.

Original

Gradient applied to rectangle

Line pattern applied to rectangle

6   Select both the placed image and the rectangle behind with a marquee-selection or the Layers palette (see "Shortcut: Select stacked objects in the Layers palette" on page 53).

7   Choose Window > Transparency and then choose Show Options from the palette menu to show all of the options. Your selected objects should appear in the thumbnail.

8   From the palette menu, choose Make Opacity Mask. To correct the image appearance, click the Invert Mask option in the Transparency palette.

Illustrator uses the placed raster image as an alpha channel for the color-filled rectangle.

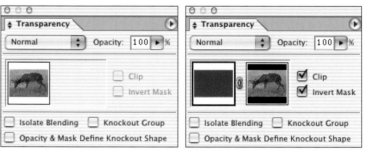

Select the rectangle and image   *Add an opacity mask*

Colorized 8-bit image

Variation: Vignette

You can also use an opacity mask to create a vignette—a soft, feathered edge—for a photo.

1   Follow the Colorized 8-bit Image technique. With the image selected, click the left thumbnail in the Transparency palette to indicate that you'll edit the vector shape. To edit the mask itself, click the right thumbnail (here, the photo).

Select the left thumbnail

2   Choose Effect > Stylize > Feather and choose a desirable amount. Turn on the Preview option to see the effect as you change the value. When you are satisfied with the vignette, click OK.

Disabling a mask

Just as in Photoshop, you can easily disable an opacity mask without deleting it by Shift-clicking the mask in the Transparency palette. Shift-click the mask thumbnail again to turn the mask back on.

Opacity mask off

Opacity mask on

Completed vignette mask

7 Transparent shadows

Designers and illustrators frequently need semitransparent shapes for shadows that overlap other objects in their drawings. The Flat-color Shadow method creates a semitransparent shadow using solid colors and the Transparency palette. It's very quick and easy. The Gradient Shadow method creates a more subtle and realistic effect using transparency, the Multiply blending mode, and a little Gaussian blur.

Shadow shape

1   Make sure that the artwork is sized, painted, and positioned as you want it.

Position the object

2   Option/Alt-click the New Layer button in the Layers palette to create a new layer. Name it Shadow. Move it directly beneath the layer of the object that will cast the shadow.

Create the Shadow layer

3   Create the shadow shape and arrange it so that it is in front of any object it shades but behind the object casting it.

Choosing a shadow color

Determine whether the light source in your illustration is warm or cool. If the light source is warm, like the example shown at left, then the shadow should be a cool hue—blue or purple. If the light source is cool, like on a foggy day, the shadow should be warm—brown or warm gray.

Flat-color shadow

1 Follow the Shadow Shape technique to create the shadow.

2 Select the shadow shape and fill it with a shadow color.

Try to use a color other than black for your shadow. It makes the shadow look more interesting and realistic. In this example, a dusty purple was used.

3 With the Shadow layer still selected, display the Transparency palette. Choose Multiply as the blending mode and adjust the opacity.

Create a colored shadow

Change the Transparency mode

4 Deselect the shadow shape and evaluate the result. If you are satisfied, save the file.

Final flat-color shadow

**Shortcut:
Adjust opacity
incrementally**

To increase or decrease the opacity by 1% increments, click the Opacity field in the Transparency palette. Press the Up Arrow key to increase the opacity and the Down Arrow key to decrease it. To increase or decrease by 10% increments, hold down Shift as you press the Up or Down Arrow key.

To create a gradated, softer shadow, try the Gradient Shadow technique that follows.

Gradient shadow

1 Follow the Shadow Shape technique to create the shadow.

2 Select the shadow shape and fill the shadow with the White, Black gradient in the Swatches palette.

3 Select the gradient tool in the toolbox. Use the tool to redirect the gradient so that the black area is closest to the object casting the shadow and the white area is farthest from the object. Make sure that the direction of the gradient matches that of the light source.

4 With the shadow shape still selected, change the blending mode to Multiply in the Transparency palette. Adjust the opacity if necessary.

Redirect the gradient

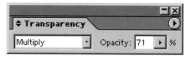

Change the blending mode

5 Choose View > Hide Edges to evaluate the adjustments without the visual distraction of the selection edges.

6 In the Gradient palette, click the black gradient slider to select it. Open the Color palette and use the palette menu to change the color mode from Grayscale to one of the color choices. Change the gradient stop from black to a different dark shadow color.

The example below used a dark purple.

7 If desired, further adjust the shadow by moving the midpoint gradient slider to change the dark and light areas of the shadow.

If you move the slider toward the the dark stop, the shadow fades more quickly. If you move the slider toward the white stop, the shadow becomes darker and fades more slowly.

Change the gradient color

Adjust the gradient midpoint

8 For a softer shadow, select the shadow shape and choose
Effect > Blur > Gaussian Blur. Use a small amount of blur to
keep the effect subtle.

If the edges don't look smooth enough, choose Effect >
Document Raster Effects Settings and increase the resolution
setting.

Final gradient shadow

8 | Asymmetrical path gradients

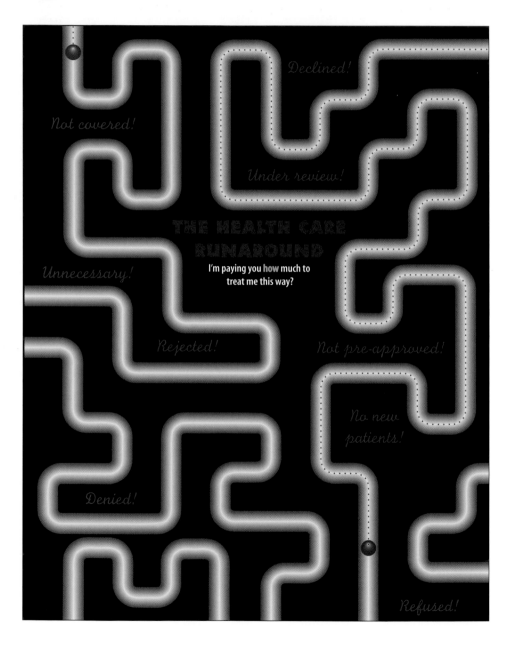

Need to create rainbows, tubes, or pipes? Then this is the technique to use. First, create an art brush from an asymmetrical gradient. (Create your own gradient or use one of the many gradients available in the swatch libraries.) Then apply it to a path. One advantage to using the art brush gradient is that you can quickly and easily change its color. Another is that if you edit the path, the gradient automatically reflows along the new path.

1   Select the rectangle tool. Position the cursor in a blank area of the file, and click once. Enter the Width and Height amounts. The Width amount should be a few times larger than the Height. The Height amount should be the thickness that you want your path gradient to be.

2   Fill the rectangle with the White, Black gradient, which is one of the default gradients found in the Swatches palette. Stroke the rectangle with None.

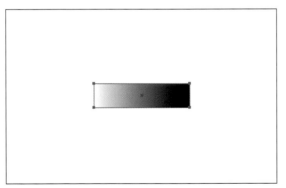

Fill the rectangle with the White, Black gradient

3   Choose Window > Gradient to display the Gradient palette. The White, Black gradient will appear in the palette. Click below the gradient bar to add a new color. Select white in the Color palette to fill the new stop with white. Position the new stop at the 70% location. If this is difficult, type in the value, and press Enter.

Finding gradients quickly

Sometimes it's hard to see which gradient is which in the Swatches and library palettes. One solution is to change the size of the swatches. The default view is small thumbnails. To change it, choose Large Thumbnail View from the palette menu. If you still need help figuring out what's what, choose List View from the palette menu.

Small Thumbnail view

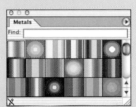

Large Thumbnail view

List view

Shortcut: Swap colors between color stops

Swap colors between color stops by Option/Alt-dragging one stop on top of another. For example, if you have white on the left and black on the right and you want to exchange them, Option/Alt-drag the white stop onto the black one. They instantly change places.

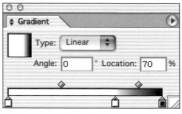

Add a new white color stop

4   Select the far right stop on the gradient bar. Select 80% black in the Color palette.

5   Select the leftmost stop on the gradient bar. Select 80% black in the Color palette. Change the angle to 90°. Press Tab to apply the change.

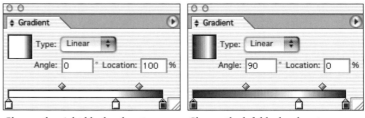

Change the right black color stop   *Change the left black color stop*

6   Evaluate the results. You should have a grayscale version of the tubular gradation that you will eventually apply to a path. If you need to resize the artwork or edit colors, do it now.

You'll expand the gradient into shapes so that you can create an art brush in the next step.

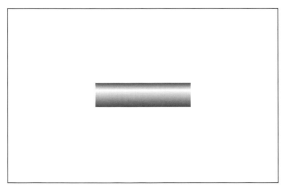

Evaluate the asymmetrical gradient

7   Choose Object > Expand to change the gradient into a series of shapes. The number of objects you specify will depend on the height of the rectangle. Click OK.

This example specified 50 objects for a 12-point thick tube. You may have to experiment with this value to create the smoothest blend. Start with a ratio of four objects for each point of tube thickness.

Expand the gradient

8   Choose Window > Pathfinder to display the Pathfinder palette. With the expanded gradient still selected, click the Crop button in the Pathfinder palette.

Expanding the gradient converts the rectangle into a mask for the blended shapes. The Crop command trims the shapes and removes the mask. Art brushes cannot contain masks.

9   Display the Brushes palette pop-up menu and make sure that Show Art Brushes is selected. Click the New Brush button at the bottom of the palette, select New Art Brush

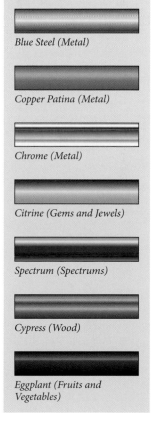

Using the gradient libraries

If you are in a hurry and don't have time to create your own gradients, try using the gradients from some of Illustrator's gradient libraries. To open them, choose Open Swatch Library from the Swatches palette menu. Choose Other Library and navigate to Adobe Illustrator CS/Presets/ Gradients. Open the gradient library of your choice. Below are just a few samples of gradients that work well as art brushes.

Blue Steel (Metal)

Copper Patina (Metal)

Chrome (Metal)

Citrine (Gems and Jewels)

Spectrum (Spectrums)

Cypress (Wood)

Eggplant (Fruits and Vegetables)

as the type, and click OK. Name the new brush, and select Tints and Shades as the Colorization method. Click OK.

Art Brush Options

Name: 12 pt tube

OK

Cancel

Direction

← → ↑ ↓

Size
Width: 100%
☐ Proportional

Flip
☐ Flip Along
☐ Flip Across

Colorization
Method: Tints and Shades
Key Color: ▉   Tips

Save the expanded gradient as an art brush

10 Create a path (or paths) to which you can apply the gradient art brush. Stroke it with the color that will be the main color of the tube gradient. Fill it with None if you want only the tube gradient to show.

Art brushes that have Colorization methods of Tints, Tints and Shades, or Hue Shift use the color of a path's stroke, not its fill.

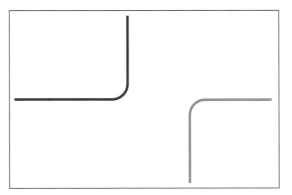

Create stroked paths

11 With the path still selected, click the gradient art brush that you just created in the Brushes palette. Save the file.

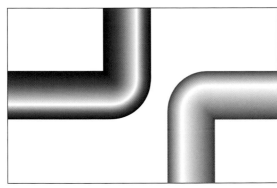

Apply the art brush to the paths

Variation: Rainbow art brush

Create a rainbow gradient art brush by replacing steps 3 through 6 of the Asymmetrical Path Gradient technique with the following:

1 Fill the rectangle with the Rainbow gradient from the default set in the Swatches palette. In the Gradient palette, change the angle to –90°.

2 Continue with steps 7 and 8.

3 When creating the art brush in step 9, use a Colorization method of None. Continue with steps 10 and 11.

Apply the rainbow art brush to the path

Fixing acute angles and corners

Corners can overlap or disconnect when paths are stroked with a thick gradient art brush. To fix mismatched corners, try reducing the brush width in the Stroke Options dialog box at the bottom of the Brushes palette. Or make the path larger. Alternatively, try this:

1 Select the shape to which the gradient art brush is applied.

2 Choose Filter > Stylize > Round Corners. Enter a value about half the width of the art brush. Click OK. If necessary, undo and try other amounts until you get the desired effect.

Original stroked shape

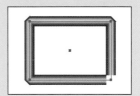

Problem corners on shape

Round Corners filter applied

Section 2 | Drawing

9 | Basic lines and shapes

You can create paths with the line and shape tools two ways. One is with the tool dialog box and the other is to click and drag with the tool. Use the following charts when you create your lines and shapes. The middle column shows the specifications for creating a path with a dialog box. The right column contains key modifiers for click-and-drag creation of shapes and lines.

Dialog box-created line or shape

1   Select a line or shape creation tool in the toolbox.

2   Either click the artboard once to open the tool dialog box; or to create the shape from its center point, Option/Alt-click once to open the tool dialog box.

3   Enter the values for your line or shape object and click OK.

Tool-drawn line or shape

1   Select a line or shape creation tool in the toolbox.

2   Either click and drag on the artboard until the path is the size you want it to be; or begin dragging, but before releasing the mouse button, use any of the modifier keys listed in the charts.

In general, the following modifier keys work for all of the line and shape creation tools:

• Shift constrains the shape or line to 45° angles or whatever constrain angle is set in your preferences.

• Spacebar halts the drawing process and lets you move the path around. Releasing the spacebar will resume the drawing process.

• Option/Alt draws the path from the reference or center point. (With the spiral tool, Option/Alt-dragging adds or subtracts winds while lengthening the spiral.)

Line or shape	Click once and specify:	Click-and-drag plus:
	Line segment tool Length = 104 points Angle = 303° Fill Line option: Off	• Option/Alt draws from the center of the line outward. • Shift constrains the line to 45° angles. • Spacebar moves the line.
	Line segment tool This effect is only produced when drawing with the tool. You cannot specify this effect in the dialog box.	` (grave accent) creates multiple line segments with their endpoints wherever you have drawn.
	Arc tool Length X-Axis = 67 points Length Y-Axis = 73 points Type: Open Base Along: Y Axis Slope = 50 Fill Arc option: Off	• Option/Alt draws from the center of the arc outward. • Shift constrains the arc to 45° angles. • Spacebar moves the arc. • C toggles between an open and closed arc. • F flips the arc while drawing. • Up Arrow or Down Arrow increases or decreases the arc's angle.
	Arc tool This effect is only produced when drawing with the tool. You cannot specify this effect in the dialog box.	` (grave accent) creates multiple line segments with their endpoints wherever you have drawn.

Line or shape	Click once and specify:	Click-and-drag plus:
	Spiral tool Radius = 45 points Decay = 80% Segments = 19 Style: Counterclockwise	• Shift constrains the spiral to 45° angles. • Spacebar moves the spiral. • Up Arrow or Down Arrow adds or deletes winds. • Option/Alt-drag adds or subtracts winds while drawing. • Moving the pointer in an arc rotates the spiral.
	Spiral tool Radius = 45 points Decay = 99% Segments = 60 Style: Counterclockwise	• Command/Control-dragging changes the decay.
	Rectangular grid tool Width = 75 points Height = 75 points Horizontal Dividers = 5, Skew = 0% Vertical Dividers = 5, Skew = 0% Use Outside Rectangle as Frame option: On Fill Grid option: Off	• Shift constrains the grid to a square. • Spacebar moves the grid. • Option/Alt draws from the center of the grid. • Up or Down Arrow adds or removes horizontal lines. • Right or Left Arrow adds or removes vertical lines. • F decreases the skew for the rows by 10%. • V increases the skew for the rows by 10%. • X decreases the skew for the columns by 10%. • C increases the skew for the columns by 10%.
	Polar grid tool Width = 75 points Height = 75 points Concentric Dividers = 5, Skew = 0% Radial Dividers = 5, Skew = 0% Create Compound Path from Ellipses option: Off Fill Grid option: Off	• Shift constrains the grid to a circle. • Spacebar moves the grid. • Option/Alt-draws from the center of the grid. • Up or Down Arrow adds or removes concentric dividers. • Right or Left Arrow adds or removes radial dividers. • X changes the skew for the concentric lines inward by 10%. • C changes the skew for the concentric dividers outward by 10%. • F changes the skew for the radial dividers counterclockwise by 10%. • V changes the skew for the radial dividers clockwise by 10%.

Line or shape	Click once and specify:	Click-and-drag plus:
	Rectangle tool Width = 86 points Height = 46 points **Rounded rectangle tool** Width = 86 points Height = 46 points Corner radius = 6 points Clicking the word Height copies the Width value and vice versa.	• Shift constrains the rectangle to a square. • Spacebar moves the rectangle. • Option/Alt draws from the center point. Rounded rectangle tool only: • Up or Down Arrow changes the corner radius. • Left Arrow changes the minimum radius (most angular corners). • Right Arrow changes the maximum radius (most rounded corners).
	Ellipse tool Width = 70 points Height = 95 points Clicking the word Height copies the Width value and vice versa.	• Shift constrains the ellipse to a circle. • Spacebar while drawing moves the ellipse. • Option/Alt draws from the center point
	Polygon tool Radius = 40 points Sides = 6	• Shift constrains the polygon to 45° angles. • Spacebar while drawing moves the polygon. • Up or Down Arrow adds or deletes sides to the polygon. • Moving the pointer in an arc rotates the polygon.
	Star tool Radius 1 = 40 points Radius 2 = 17.6 points Points = 5	• Shift constrains the star to 45° angles. • Spacebar while drawing moves the star. • Up or Down Arrow adds or deletes sides to the star. • Moving the pointer in an arc rotates the star. • Command/Ctrl holds the inner radius constant. • Option/Alt keeps the sides of the star straight.

10 | Reverse shapes

Overlapping type and graphics is a hallmark of Art Deco graphic design. You can use these techniques, however, for any overlapping shapes whose colors you want to change at the point where the shapes overlap. Start with a background element and the objects or type that will reverse out of it. If you want to be able to move the shapes after creating the reversed effect, use the Two-tone Reverse Shapes technique. If you want to paint shapes with different colors, use the Multitone Reverse Shapes technique.

Two-tone reverse shapes

1   Create the background element of your design.

Keep in mind that the paint attributes of the backmost object will be adopted by the other objects in the compound path.

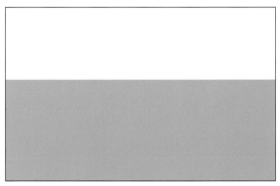

Create the background element

2   Create the objects or type that will reverse out of the background element. Position them as you want them in the final design.

Reversing compound paths

Here's how to fix a self-intersecting compound path or change the way some of its shapes reverse:

1 Select a compound path.

2 Choose Window > Attributes. In the palette, click the Non-Zero Winding Rule and Reverse Path Direction Off buttons.

3 To reverse a shape within a compound path, select the shape with the direct selection tool. Click the Reverse Path Direction On button.

Create the type that will reverse

3 If you are not using type as an element, skip this step. If you are using type, select it and choose Type > Create Outlines.

4 Select the background element and the foreground type or elements. Choose Object > Compound Path > Make.

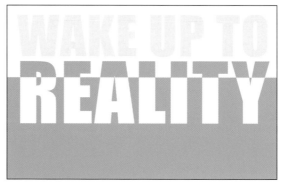

Create a compound path

5 Deselect everything and check your work. Place an element behind the compound path, and notice that you can see through the "holes" that were created in the background element of the compound shape.

In this example, a yellow circle was placed behind the compound path.

Create an object behind the compound path

6 Use the group selection tool to adjust elements of the compound path. To select an element, click its edge. To select a compound element, like the *A* in the illustration, click the edge of the element twice with the group-selection tool.

You can move, reshape, or transform the objects within the compound path. However, changing an object's color updates the entire compound path.

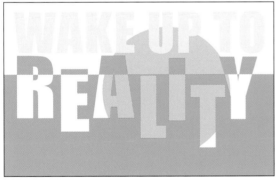

Move elements within the compound path

Alternating holes

If your compound path doesn't have its holes in the right places, you may need to change the way Illustrator interprets the relationship of the shapes. Here's how to make every other shape a hole:

1 Select the shapes and choose Object > Compound Path > Make.

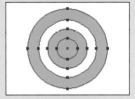

Apply the Compound Path command

2 Choose Window > Attributes to display the Attributes palette.

Select Even-Odd Fill Rule

3 With the compound path still selected, click the Even-Odd Fill Rule button.

Completed artwork

Predicting pathfinder results

Use these illustrations to help predict the results of using the Pathfinder palette buttons.

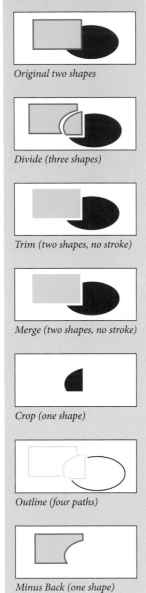

Original two shapes

Divide (three shapes)

Trim (two shapes, no stroke)

Merge (two shapes, no stroke)

Crop (one shape)

Outline (four paths)

Minus Back (one shape)

Multitone reverse shapes

1   Create the background element of your design.

The paint attributes of this object will change to that of the topmost object after you use the Pathfinder command in step 4.

Create the background element

2   Create the objects or type that will reverse out of the background element. Position them as you want them in relation to the background element; after step 4, you won't be able to readjust the position of the elements.

Create the type that will reverse

3   If you are not using type as an element, skip this step. If you are using type, select it and choose Type > Create Outlines.

4 Select the background element and the foreground type or elements. Choose Window > Pathfinder to display the Pathfinder palette. Option/Alt-click the Exclude button.

Using Option/Alt with the Exclude button expands the artwork into separate shapes at the same time. Not expanding the artwork when using the Pathfinder palette creates only a compound shape. In this case, you want separate shapes.

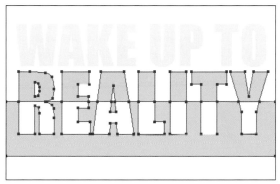

Use Exclude to create separate shapes

5 Use the direct selection tool to select the objects you want to repaint, and change them as desired.

Each remaining area of color is now a separate object, and you no longer can move the original artwork elements. The overlapping areas that look white are actually "holes" in the artwork.

Repaint selected objects

Predicting shape mode results

Use these illustrations to help predict the results of using the Shape Mode buttons in the Pathfinder palette.

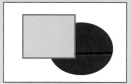

Original artwork

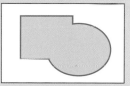

Add to Shape Area mode

Subtract from Shape Area mode

Intersect Shape Areas mode

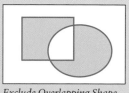

Exclude Overlapping Shape Areas mode

11 | Custom borders

One of the most useful things you can create with the Adobe Illustrator pattern brush is a border. Pattern brushes give you the option of varying the corner design from the side design. You don't have to worry about calculating the size of the tile to fit your particular rectangle because Illustrator offers three Pattern Brush fit options. If you want to customize one of the pattern brushes provided in the several libraries that come with Illustrator, simply drag the tiles from the Brushes palette onto the artboard and change the artwork to your taste. Then follow steps 7 through 14 to resave the tiles.

Copying objects and constraining transformations

Pressing Option or Alt while you transform an object leaves a copy of the original behind. Pressing Shift while transforming an object constrains the transformation to a 90° or 45° angle.

1   Select the rectangle tool and create a square large enough to contain the border corner artwork.

It doesn't matter what the fill and stroke are because this square will become a guide.

2   Choose View > Hide Bounding Box. With the selection tool, click one of the left corner points and drag the square to the right, pressing Shift+Option/Alt as you drag. When the left corner point aligns with the right one, release the mouse button and then Shift and Option/Alt to create a copy.

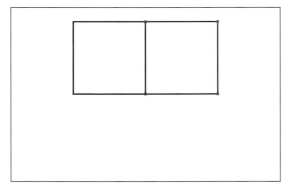

Create a rectangle and Shift+Option/Alt–drag to duplicate it

3 Select both of the squares. Click one of the corner top points, press Shift+Option/Alt, and drag the squares straight down. When the top corner point aligns with the bottom one, release the mouse button and then Shift and Option/Alt to create copies.

4 Select all four of the squares and choose View > Guides > Make Guides.

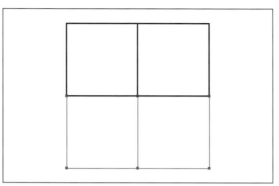

Duplicate the two rectangles

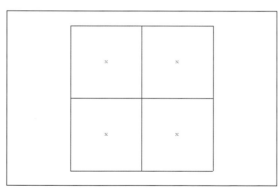

Make the rectangles into guides

5 Create the artwork for the sides of the border in the upper right square guide.

The artwork should be just shapes or lines. If you use a brush stroke, expand it first so that you can use its points to align to the edges and center point of the pattern tile boundaries. Don't use unexpanded brush strokes because aligning them perfectly is nearly impossible.

6   Select the rectangle tool and create a square the same size as the square guide. Fill and stroke the square with None. Choose Object > Arrange > Send to Back.

This invisible square will become the bounding box for the side pattern tile. It will also help you align the side tile with the corner tile.

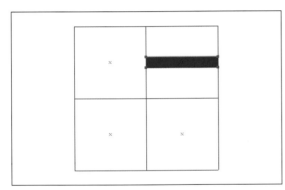

Create the border side artwork

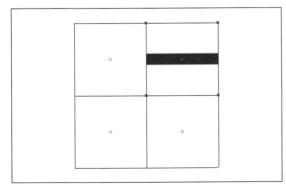

Create the bounding box for the border side artwork

Controlling the edge of the border and path

To match the outside edge of your border with the outside edge of your path, create the side and corner artwork inside (below and to the right) of the center point of the bounding boxes. If you center the artwork, the border will straddle the path: half the border design will fall inside of the path, and half outside. Check your work by drawing a path and painting it with the border pattern brush.

Matching border and path outside edges

Border pattern brush applied

To have the border fall outside of the artwork, create the border artwork above and to the left of the bounding boxes.

7   Select both the side artwork and its invisible bounding box. Choose New Brush from the Brushes palette menu. Select New Pattern Brush as the type, and click OK. The side tile artwork will appear in the Side Tile thumbnail. To keep the border the same color, choose None for the Colorization method. Name the tile and click OK.

Create the border side artwork

8   Choose Illustrator > Preferences > Smart Guides & Slices (Mac OS X) or Edit > Preferences > Smart Guides & Slices (Windows) to set the Display options. Turn on all of the Display options. Then choose View > Smart Guides and make sure that they are turned on.

You need to use guides to ensure that the tile art and corner art align perfectly.

9   With the side tile artwork still selected, select the reflect tool in the toolbox. Click once on the bottom left corner of the selected artwork (1). Press Option/Alt and click a second time on the upper left corner of the top left guide box (2) to create a copy.

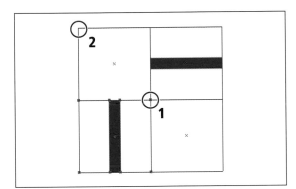

Reflect the horizontal side to create the vertical side.

10   Create the corner artwork. Use the Smart Guides' Text Label Hints, Object Highlighting, and Construction Guides options as aids in matching the points of the outer corner design to the side tile design. The side tiles should flow seamlessly into the outer corner tile.

11   Repeat step 6 to create an invisible bounding box for the outer corner design.

Dealing with extreme angles

Some wide or multiline pattern brushes can do unpredictable things when applied to a shape with wide or acute angles. To neaten corners, you can try a couple of things. First, try reducing the pattern brush size by clicking the Options of Selected Object button in the Brushes palette and changing the scale. If you want to keep the pattern brush the same size, try selecting the path and choosing Filter > Stylize > Rounded Corners. Enter a radius amount and click OK. This usually takes care of the problem.

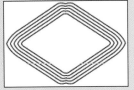

Angled corners

Rounded Corners filter applied

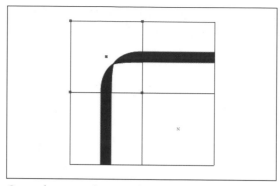

Create the corner design and its bounding box

12 To define the outer corner design artwork as a pattern brush, select the outer corner tile artwork and its bounding box. Option/Alt-drag it into the Brushes palette and position it over the outer corner section of the new pattern brush that you created in step 7. When a thick black border appears, release the mouse button and then Option/Alt. Click OK in the Pattern Brush Options dialog box.

13 To define the inner corner design artwork as a pattern brush, repeat step 12 for the inner corner design, except Option/Alt-drag the design into the inner corner section in the Brushes palette. Usually the outer corner design also works as the inner corner design. To create an inner corner for asymmetric borders, return to step 10. Rotate the outer corner tile art 90° and adjust it to match the side tile. Continue with step 11-12; then skip to step 14.

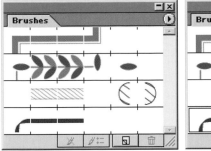 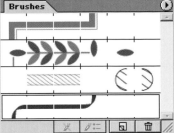

Define the outer corner design *Define the inner corner design*

14 Once you've defined the sides and corners of the pattern brush, test it. Draw a shape and click the pattern brush name in the Brushes palette.

Notice in the example that shapes without corners, such as a circle, are painted only with the side tile design. Corner tiles appear only on paths with corner points.

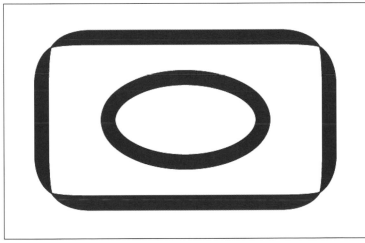

Apply pattern brush to create border

12 | Scalloped seals

Why add anchor points?

You get different effects when you use the Distort filters if you add anchor points to your shape first. This is especially true of simple objects that don't have a lot of points to begin with. Compare the different results below. Both circles below were distorted by 38% using the Pucker & Bloat filter.

4-point circle

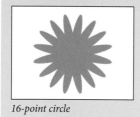

16-point circle

You can create a scalloped seal in Illustrator two ways: using the scallop tool or the Pucker & Bloat filter. The results for each differ slightly. The Pucker & Bloat filter lets you preview the effect. The scallop tool is more immediate but gives you less control over the results.

Scalloped seals circle

1   Select the ellipse tool, hold down Shift, and draw a circle. Holding down Shift as you draw creates a circle.

2   If you'll use the Scalloped Tool method, look at the Info palette and note the diameter (W or H value) of the circle.

Pucker & Bloat filter

1   Choose Object > Path > Add Anchor Points. Reapply the Add Anchor Points command as needed until you have the number of points you want.

In the example, the command was applied three times.

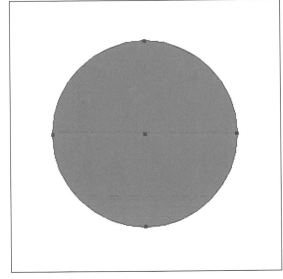

Create a circle

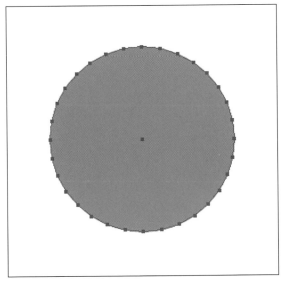

Add anchor points

2 Choose Filter > Distort > Pucker & Bloat. Select the Preview option and enter a negative number to position the points on the outer edge of the circle. Click OK.

In the example, a value of –5% was used.

Apply the Pucker & Bloat filter

Scallop tool

1 Double-click the scallop tool (under the warp tool). Enter a width and height for the brush size that is 12 points larger than the circle. Set the Intensity to 20% and Complexity to 8.

2 Click the scallop tool cross hair on the center of the circle. Continue to hold down the mouse button to add scallops. The longer you press the mouse button, the more extreme the result.

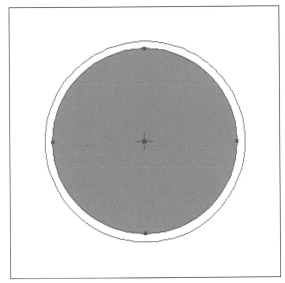

Center the scallop tool on the circle

Hold down the mouse button as needed

13 | Three-dimensional stars

Drawing paths on top of other paths

When you are trying to align paths or points on paths, it helps to use the Snap to Point and Smart Guides features. If you are trying to draw a new path directly on top of another path, first be sure to deselect the path below. Notice that if you position the pen tool on top of a point on a selected path, the pointer changes to the delete anchor point tool. If the path is deselected before you start to draw, the Smart Guides will indicate that the pointer is on top of an anchor point by displaying the word "anchor." Once the path is deselected, the pen tool cursor will appear when positioned over the other path's anchor point.

This technique uses a combination of Illustrator commands to create a quick three-dimensional star.

1   Select the star tool, and click once in the document. Enter 4 in the Points field, and click OK. Choose Select > Deselect.

This example used a value of 40 points for Radius 1 and 20 points for Radius 2.

2   Using the View menu, turn on the Smart Guides and Snap to Point commands. Select the pen tool, and draw horizontal, vertical, and diagonal lines across the star between the anchor points. Use the Smart Guides to help you locate the anchor points.

It's a good idea to stroke the lines with a contrasting color to check alignment. The stroke color will disappear in the next step.

Create a 4-pointed star

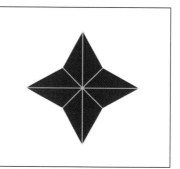

Draw straight lines using anchor points as guides

3   Choose Window > Pathfinder to display the Pathfinder palette. Select the star and all the intersecting lines. Click the Divide button in the Pathfinder palette to slice the star into separate shapes.

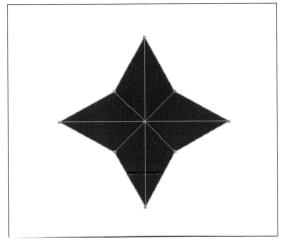

Divide the star into separate shapes

4 Select the direct selection tool, hold down Shift, and select every other triangle in the star. Fill them with contrasting colors.

For best results, use a dark color for the shaded areas and a lighter value for the highlighted areas. To change color saturation quickly, in the Color palette hold down Shift as you drag a CMYK or RGB slider.

Pathfinder palette vs. Pathfinder effects

What's the difference between using the Pathfinder filters in the Pathfinder palette and using the Pathfinder filters in the Effects menu? Basically, it's editability.

Use the Pathfinder palette on selected paths or shapes to produce a compound path, grouped paths, or just a final path. However, you won't be able to go back and edit, change, or remove the effect later.

Use the Pathfinder filters in the Effects menu on groups, layers, or sublayers. You can change or remove the pathfinder effect at any time because it is a live effect.

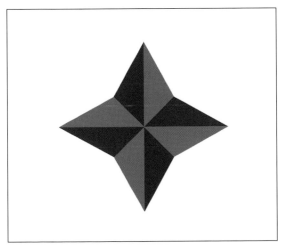

Paint alternate shapes with different values

14 | Interlocking stroked objects

Nudging your paths

Sometimes it's hard to move shapes by small amounts without zooming way in. And when you zoom in, you often lose sight of the other objects in your file. You can move selected objects with the arrow keys on your keyboard. Set the increment amount by choosing Illustrator > Preferences > General (Mac OS X) or Edit > Preferences > General (Windows) and entering an amount in the Keyboard Increment text box. The default value is set to 1 point. Change it to whatever you want. You can even set it as low as 0.001 point. By holding down Option/Alt each time you click the arrow key, you can leave a copy behind.

It's difficult to overlap stroked shapes because the strokes often outline areas that shouldn't be stroked. You'll use the Pathfinder palette to create interlocking shapes with natural-looking strokes.

1   Position the objects that you want to link. Once you complete step 2, you won't be able to move them in relation to each other any more. Select the objects that you want to link. Don't worry about adding the stroke yet—you'll do it at the end.

2   With the objects still selected, choose Window > Pathfinder to display the Pathfinder palette. Click the Divide button to define the overlapping color areas as separate shapes.

Create the objects to be linked

Use the Divide button to create overlap shapes

Creating and expanding compound paths

The Shape Mode buttons in the Pathfinder palette create compound paths. You may want to expand a compound path to access some of the Pathfinder-created shapes. To create a compound path and expand it at the same time, hold down Option/Alt as you click a Shape Mode button.

3 Determine how the links should be arranged visually to create the interlocking effect. With the direct selection tool, Shift-select the shapes you want to fill with one color. Click the Add to Shape Area button in the Pathfinder palette to join the selected shapes into one shape. Paint it with the appropriate color.

4 While the shape is still selected, click the Expand button in the Pathfinder palette.

This creates a shape that can be stroked in the next step.

Expand the compound paths

Add overlap shapes to links

5 Repeat steps 3 and 4 for all interlocking objects in your artwork. Adjust the fill and stroke attributes of the objects.

Add the stroke to the links

Predicting the results of the Pathfinder filters

These illustrations give you an idea of what to expect when you use the Pathfinder palette. To use the Pathfinder palette, select two or more objects and click a palette button. Shapes buttons create a compound path; clicking the Expand button makes the Shapes operation permanent. Pathfinder buttons don't create a compound shape and their results cannot be expanded or released.

Shapes:

Original artwork (two shapes)

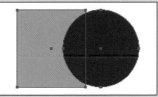
Original artwork (shapes overlapped)

Add to Shape Area*: *Combines shapes into one shape*

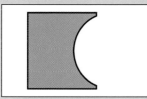
Subtract From Shape Area*: *Leaves top shape and area where it overlaps other shapes*

Intersect Shape Areas*: *Leaves only the intersecting area*

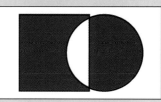
Exclude Overlapping Shape Areas*: *Leaves a hole (a compound shape) where areas intersect*

Pathfinders:

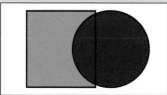
Divide*: *Creates a separate shape for every area of overlap*

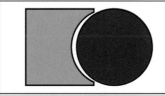
Trim*: *Removes any hidden part of a shape*

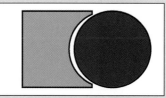
Merge*: *Removes any hidden part of a shape and merges adjoining or overlapping shapes of the same color*

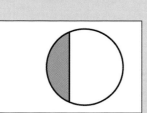
Crop*: *Crops shapes outside the area of of the top object, which is filled and stroked with None*

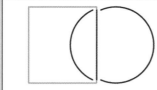
Outline: *Divides objects into line segments*

Minus Back*: *Removes the backmost object and shape areas that overlap it*

*Filter results are outlined in black to emphasize the resulting shape edges.

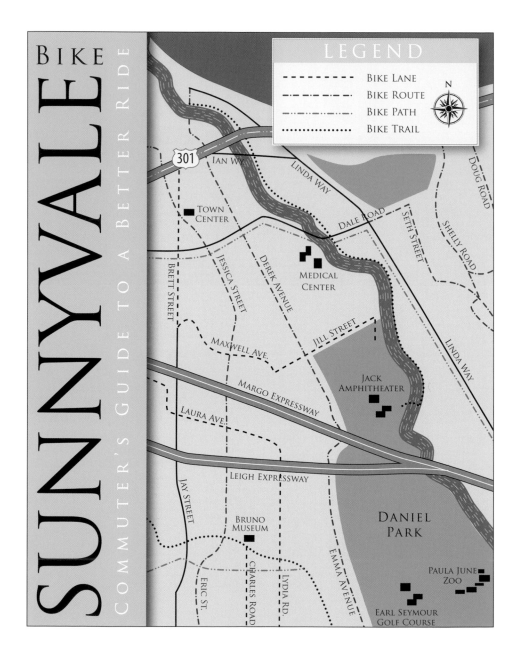

You can generate a variety of useful and decorative line effects for maps by varying the dash patterns of lines and using the Appearance palette to layer them. Use the following technique to create a layered line. Then use the Line Effect Settings chart on pages 102 and 103 to create different types of line effects. Save the line effects as graphic styles and then as a style library so that you can use the effects in other images.

1   Use the pen tool to draw the path for the line effect.

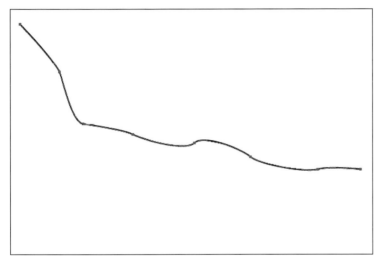

Create a path

2   With the path still selected, choose Window > Appearance to display the Appearance palette. Select the Stroke item in the Appearance list.

3   In the Color palette, change the stroke's color. In the Stroke palette (Window > Stroke), change its weight to the widest amount that you want your line to be. This will be the outside edge of the line.

In the following example the stroke weight was changed to 4 points.

Scaling multiple-stroke appearances

Strokes in multistroke appearances, like the one shown in this technique, can be scaled two ways.

First, to scale the path and scale the stroke appearance with it, choose Illustrator > Preferences > General (Mac OS X) or Edit > Preferences > General (Windows) and turn on the Scale Strokes & Effects option. Scaling the path also scales the appearance.

To scale just the appearance, select each stroke in the Appearance palette and change the stroke weight and dash amounts in the Stroke palette by the same percentage. For example, reduce the appearance by half by multiplying each stroke weight and dash amount by 50%.

Original appearance

Strokes and dashes reduced by 50%

Applying a graphic style to a layer

When making maps, a time-saving technique is to apply a style to a layer so that you don't have to apply it to each individual path. A benefit of this method is that you can change the way paths look when they overlap each other.

The top illustration shows both paths have a style applied to them. Notice how the area of intersection looks. To add a style to a layer, click the target circle for that layer in the Layers palette. Then click the graphic style you want in the Graphic Styles palette. Everything created on that layer will have that style.

Each path has a style applied

Target the layer and add the graphic style

Layer has a style applied

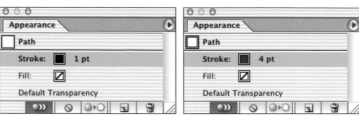

Select the Stroke item

Change the stroke color and weight

4 From the Appearance palette menu, choose Add New Stroke. Change the color and stroke weight.

In the following example the stroke weight was changed to 3 points and painted 50% black.

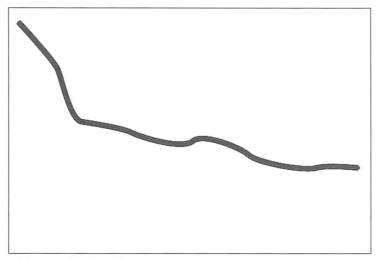

Add a second stroke to the appearance

5 Repeat step 4 for the desired number of strokes on the path. Remember that each stroke used will be partially covered by the strokes added above it in the Appearance palette list.

6 To create a dashed line, select the Dashed Line option in the Stroke palette. (If needed, choose Show Options from the Stroke palette menu.) Enter a value in the first text box; adjust the Line Cap options as desired. To vary the dashed pattern, vary the text box values; see "Line Effect Settings" on pages 102 and 103 for more information.

This example shows the third stroke changed to a 0.5-point dashed white line.

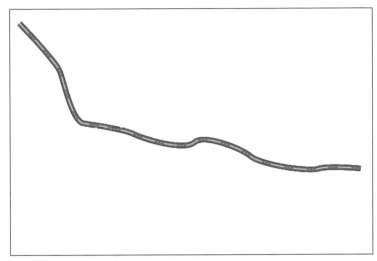

Add a third stroke to the appearance

7   Save the completed line effect as a graphic style for reuse on other lines. With the line still selected, Option/Alt-click the New Style button at the bottom of the Graphic Styles palette. Name the style and click OK.

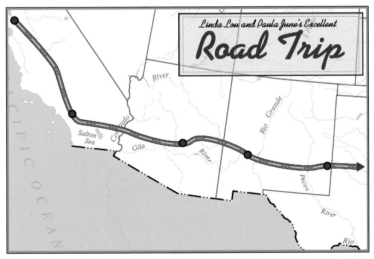

Completed illustration

Creating a graphic style library

When you have several styles in a file that you want to use in other files, save those styles in a style library. That library can be opened up and used with any other file you open in Illustrator.

To save a style:

1   In the Graphic Styles palette, choose Save Graphic Style Library from the palette menu.

2   In the Save dialog box that appears, name the file and navigate to Adobe Illustrator CS/Presets/Graphic Styles. Click Save.

To use the library:

1   From the Graphic Styles palette menu, choose Open Graphic Style Library and then choose Other Library.

2   In the Open dialog box that appears, navigate to Adobe Illustrator CS/Presets/Graphic Styles. Find the file you saved and click Open. The styles will now be available for use.

Line Effect Settings

Effect*	Stroke Color	Stroke Weight (points)	Line Cap	Dash Pattern
	100% Black	2	Round	0, 2
	100% Black	2	Round	0, 4
	100% Black	2	Round	0, 10
	100% Black	2	Projecting	0, 4
	100% Black	2	Projecting	0, 10
	100% Black	2	Round	20, 10, 0, 10
	100% Black	2	Round	10, 5, 0, 5, 10, 12
	100% Black	2	Round	8, 4.5, 0, 4.5, 0, 4.5
	100% Black	2	Round	15, 4, 0, 4, 0, 4
	100% Black	8	Butt	0.3, 9
	100% Black	5	Butt	0.5, 9
	100% Black	10	Butt	0.5, 28
	White	10	Projecting	0, 20
	100% Black	12	Projecting	0, 20
	100% Black	8	Projecting	0, 20
	White	10	Projecting	0, 20
	100% Black	12	Projecting	0, 20
	100% Black	4	Projecting	0, 20
	White	5	Projecting	0, 20
	100% Black	6	Projecting	Not dashed

Multiple listings denote multiple layers in corresponding order in the Appearance palette.

Line Effect Settings

Effect*	Stroke Color	Stroke Weight (points)	Line Cap	Dash Pattern
	100% Black	6	Butt	10, 10
	20% Black	6	Butt	Not dashed
	100% Black	8	Butt	Not dashed
	Green	6	Butt	18, 54, 18, 54, 18, 54
	Cyan	6	Butt	36, 36, 36, 36, 36, 36
	Dark blue	6	Butt	54, 18, 54, 18, 54, 18
	Orange	6	Butt	Not dashed
	Black	7	Butt	Not dashed
	White	1	Butt	Not dashed
	20% Black	6	Butt	Not dashed
	100% Black	8	Butt	Not dashed
	Yellow	1	Butt	6, 4.5, 6, 4.5, 6, 4.5
	50% Black	8	Butt	Not dashed
	100% Black	10	Butt	Not dashed
	White	.5	Butt	4, 3, 5, 2, 6, 7
	Aqua	3	Butt	Not dashed
	White	4	Butt	2, 3, 4, 7, 1.5, 4
	Aqua	7	Butt	Not dashed
	White	8	Butt	6, 4.5, 3, 5, 7, 2
	Aqua	10	Butt	Not dashed
	Black	4	Butt	2, 4
	White	4	Butt	Not dashed
	Black	5	Butt	Not dashed
	White	6	Butt	Not dashed
	Black	7	Butt	Not dashed
	Black	12	Butt	2, 4
	White	5	Butt	4, 4
	Black	7.5	Butt	Not dashed
	White	13	Butt	4, 4
	Black	12.5	Butt	Not dashed

Multiple listings denote multiple layers in corresponding order in the Appearance palette.

16 | Map symbols

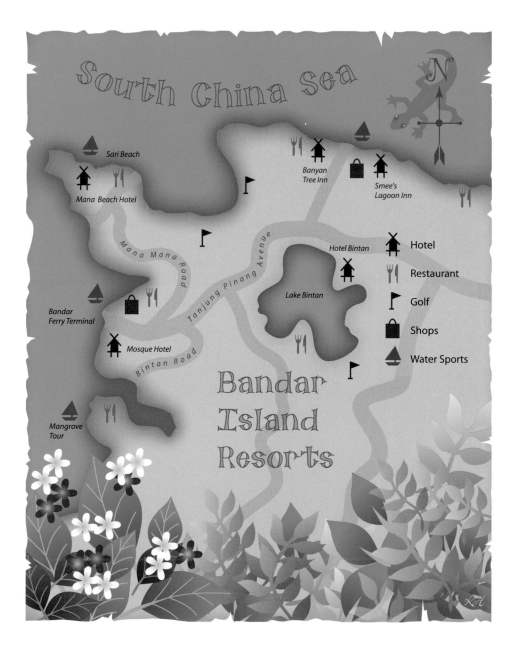

Here's a real time-saver for mapmakers—or anyone using duplicates of the same artwork. Use the Symbols palette for maps or any illustrations that require several copies of the same artwork. You simply place as many instances of a symbol as you want. The advantage to using symbols is that you can make changes quickly and easily to all the symbols in the file at once. Or you can select and change individual symbol instances without affecting all the others. Once you've mastered using the Symbols palette here, try the Foliage technique on page 128 for another way to use symbols.

Shortcut: Create and name a symbol

With the symbol artwork selected, Option/Alt-click the New Symbol button in the Symbols palette to open the Symbol Options dialog box. Type in the name. You have just created and named a new symbol in one mouse click.

1   Create a symbol or graphic that you want to repeat several times on your map. Select the symbol artwork.

2   Choose Window > Symbols to display the Symbols palette. Drag the selected artwork onto the Symbols palette. When you see the thick, black border inside the palette, release the mouse button.

3   Double-click the symbol to open the Symbol Options dialog box, and name the new symbol. Click OK.

Create the symbol graphic

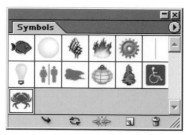

Add the graphic to the Symbols palette

4   Open or create your illustration. Make it the Background
layer of your artwork.

Open your illustration

5   Click the Place Symbol Instance button at the bottom of
the Symbols palette. This places one symbol instance in the
center of your window.

If you want to control exactly where the symbol is placed, drag
the symbol from the Symbols palette onto the artwork directly.

Place a symbol instance

6 Continue placing symbols in each place you want the symbol to appear. Save the file. If you want to edit the symbol, continue with the next step.

You can also Option/Alt-drag and move an existing symbol instance in the artwork to make a copy and leave the original behind.

Place the remaining symbol instances

Organizing your map symbols

Typically mapmakers need to use several different types of symbols in their artwork. You can easily find the symbols you want if you set up your Symbols palette before you start. From the Symbols palette pop-up menu, choose either Small List View or Large List View. Each time you create a new symbol, be sure to name it.

The palette arrranges symbols in the order in which they were created. Rearrange them by dragging the name of the symbol. When you see a heavy black line between two symbols in the list, release the mouse button to place it there.

Symbol editing

1   Select one of the symbol instances in your artwork.

2   Click the Break Link to Symbol button at the bottom of the Symbols palette.

You can use the transform tools on a symbol instance or perform operations in the Appearance, Transparency, or Styles palette without breaking the link. But you can't edit the paths or change the colors without breaking the link.

Select a symbol instance

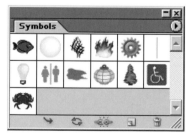

Break the link to the symbol

3   Create the new or altered symbol.

This example shows the color of the crab changed.

Create the new symbol

4 To replace the symbol with the newly edited version, select the new or altered symbol. Then select the original symbol in the Symbols palette, and choose Redefine Symbol from the Symbols palette menu.

The symbol is changed and all of its instances are updated with the new symbol.

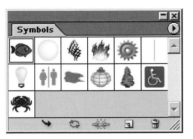

Replace the old symbol with the new

5 Save the file. If you are satisfied with your artwork, continue adding symbols. If you want to edit individual symbol instances, continue with the next step.

Creating your own library

Don't be misled by the word "symbol." You can make a symbol out of lots of things. Because of this, you can create libraries of objects, text, or images that you use all the time. After you place symbols, you can alter them or break the link. Here are some things that might be part of your library:

- A company logo
- Addresses
- Copy blocks
- Web page buttons
- Arrows
- Frames
- Legal text
- Spot illustrations

Illustration with updated symbols

Symbol-instance editing

1   Select one of the symbol instances in your artwork. Zoom in on the artwork, if necessary.

2   Use any of the transform tools, or perform an operation in the Appearance, Transparency, or Styles palette on the symbol instance.

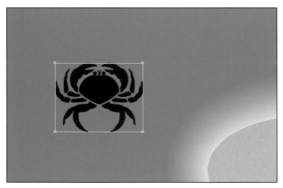

Select the symbol graphic

Any of these operations can be performed on a symbol instance without breaking its link to the original symbol. In this example, the symbol instance was scaled and its opacity was set to 25%.

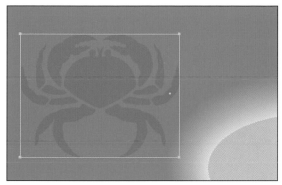

Change the symbol instance

3   When you are satisfied with the changes, save the file.

Illustration with edited symbol instances

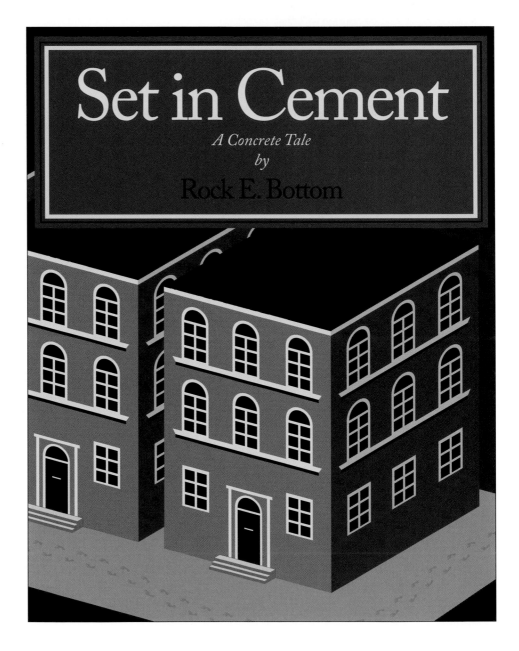

When you need to make custom projected drawings and the 3D Effects feature doesn't suit your needs, use Illustrator's precision tools to create isometric, axonometric, dimetric, and trimetric views from your two-dimensional artwork. The chart on page 119 at the end of this technique provides the precise values needed for each type of three-dimensional drawing.

1   Use the View menu to turn on the Snap to Point and Smart Guides options. In the Layers palette, create a new layer named Front. Create a flat front view of your object.

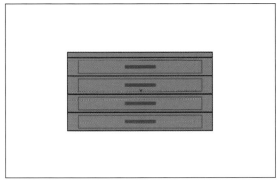

Create the front view of the object

2   In the Layers palette, create a new layer named Side. Create a flat side view of your object.

3   In the Layers palette, create a new layer named Top. Create a flat top view of your object.

4   Look at the "3D and Corresponding Flat Views" chart on page 115 and determine which view you want to create. Place the top and side in relation to the front so that it matches the illustration in the chart. Use the Smart Guides and Snap to Point features to align the corners at the intersection point.

The three views will be scaled, sheared, and rotated using the intersection point as the point of origin.

Dividing a rectangle into equal segments

When creating architectural-type drawings—for example, a wall with wood paneling, a tile floor, or a chest of drawers—you often need a larger rectangle divided into several equal rectangular segments. This can be done easily with Illustrator's Split Into Grid feature. Here's how:

1   Select the rectangle and choose Object > Path > Split Into Grid.

Create a rectangle

2   If you want horizontal segments, change the Rows number. If you want no space between the segments, set the Gutter amount to 0. Click OK.

Rows
Number: 3
Height: 17.67 pt
Gutter: 0 pt
Total: 53 pt

Enter the number of segments

Rectangle divided into three

Drawing at an angle

If you want to draw and move objects at an angle, you can change the constrain angle to help you. To change the angle, choose Illustrator > Preferences > General (Mac OS X) or Edit > Preferences > General (Windows). Enter the new constrain angle and click OK.

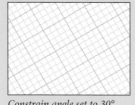

Constrain angle set to 30° and grid turned on

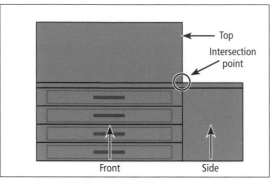

Create the side and top views of the object

5   Select the top panel by clicking in the Layers palette to the right of the target circle of the Top layer. Select the scale tool in the toolbox, and Option/Alt-click the intersection point to set the point of origin. The Scale dialog box opens.

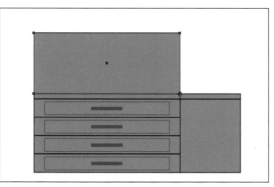

Select the top view using the Layers palette

3D and Corresponding Flat Views

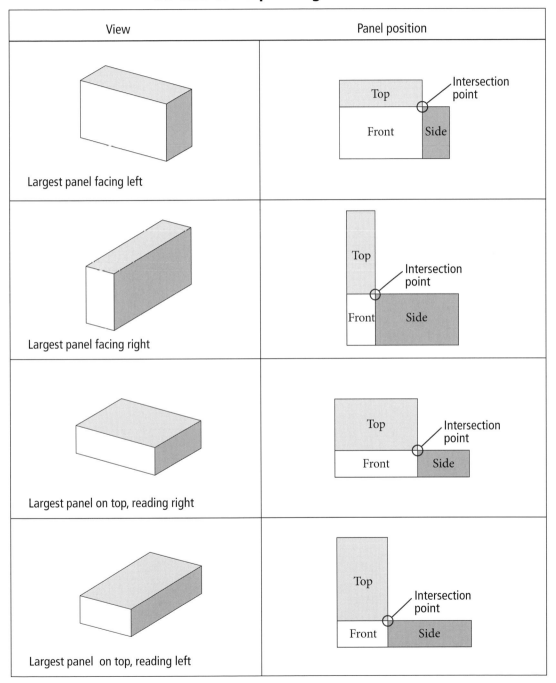

6 Click the Non-Uniform Scale option and enter the appropriate Vertical scale value for the top panel from the "3D View and Transformation Values" chart on page 119. Click OK.

This example used values for the Trimetric 2 view, with a Vertical scale of 70.711%.

Scale the top vertically

7 With the top panel still selected, select the shear tool and Option/Alt-click the intersection point. Enter the appropriate value for Horizontal Shear from the chart on the facing page.

This example used 45°.

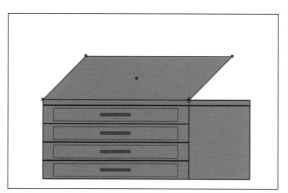

Shear the top panel

8 Select the rotate tool, and Option/Alt-click the intersection point. Enter the rotate value indicated in the chart, and click OK.

This step makes the top panel appear to recede into space. In this example, the rotation angle was –15°.

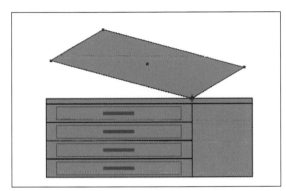

Rotate the top panel

9 Repeat steps 5 through 8 for the front panel, using the same intersection point. Be sure to use the numbers indicated for the front panel in the "3D View and Transformation Values" chart on page 119.

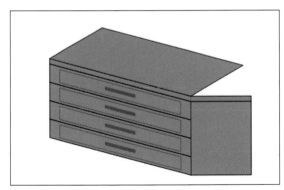

Transform the front panel

10 Repeat steps 5 through 8 for the side panel, using the same intersection point and the corresponding set of numbers in the "3D View and Transformation Values" chart on page 119.

Scaling with or without the bounding box

It's handy to use the bounding box of a shape for quick transformations, but very limited for transforming around an intersection point. Scaling with a bounding box limits you to nine points about which you can scale the object. The illustration here shows eight points; the ninth point is the center point.

The scale tool lets you click anywhere to set the point of origin. This is infinitely more useful when creating technical drawings.

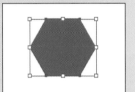

Bounding box turned on and the selection tool selected

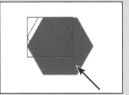

Scaling with 1 of 9 points

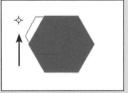

Scale tool sets the origin point anywhere

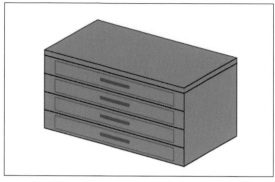

Transform the side panel

11 If the panels are stroked, zoom in very close on the corner joints to see whether the corners extend past the intersection point, as shown in this illustration. Identify which panels have this problem.

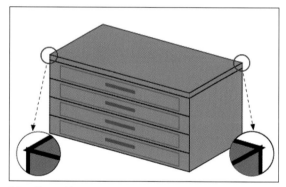

Identify problem corners

12 To fix the corners, use the direct selection tool to select the panel edges; then select the Round Join option in the Stroke palette. To enhance the three-dimensional effect, paint the panels with slightly different shades and tints. Save the file.

This example shows the colors lightened on the top panel and darkened on the side panel. To do this see the "Shortcut: Lighten or darken a CMYK color" on page 45.

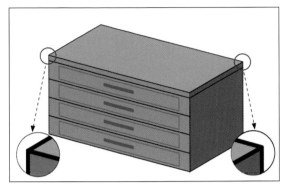

Change the strokes to round joins

3D View and Transformation Values

View Style			Vertical Scale	Horizontal Shear	Rotate
Axonometric		Top	100%	0°	−45°
		Front	70.711%	−45°	−45°
		Side	70.711%	45°	45°
Isometric		Top	86.602%	30°	−30°
		Front	86.602%	30°	30°
		Side	86.602%	30°	30°
Dimetric		Top	96.592%	15°	−15°
		Front	96.592%	−15°	−15°
		Side	50.000%	60°	60°
Trimetric 1		Top	86.602%	30°	−15°
		Front	96.592%	−15°	−15°
		Side	70.711%	45°	45°
Trimetric 2		Top	70.711%	45°	−15°
		Front	96.592%	−15°	−15°
		Side	86.602%	30°	30°

18 | Perspective drawing

This technique shows how to use guidelines and Smart Guides to create perspective drawings. You'll set up the perspective grid and create the flat shapes that appear on the picture plane. Then you'll draw the sides of the objects along the grid lines and create any receding copies of the elements within the object using the scale tool. The final steps in the technique show how to create blends for repeating horizontal or vertical details.

Objects in perspective

1 Create a simple 1-point perspective grid. First draw a rectangle to denote the picture plane (A) and a horizon line (B). Then decide where the vanishing point (C) will be. Draw straight lines from the vanishing point past the corners of the rectangle. The lines should intersect the corners of the picture plane.

2 Select the lines and rectangle and choose View > Guides > Make Guides.

Shortcut: Create a guide layer

The Layers palette is a great place to edit, lock, unlock, hide, and show guides. Create all your guides on one layer, called Guide Layer. You can name the guides and hide or show them when needed. If you want to be able to move them around as well, choose View > Guides > Lock Guides to unlock the guides. Then you can lock and unlock individual guides as needed in the Layers palette. Remember that if you unlock your guides, they will be selectable and can be moved. You probably want to keep them locked unless you are editing them.

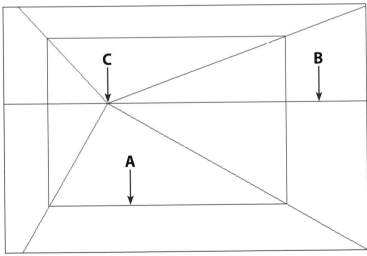

Create simple 1-point perspective guides

3 Create the background shapes. Remember to use the horizon line (B) guide when creating the sky and earth or floors and walls.

Changing the guide color

The default color for guides is cyan. If you can't see this color because of the colors in your image, you can change it to a different, more contrasting color.

Press Command/Ctrl+K to open the Preferences dialog box. Choose Guides & Grid from the pop-up menu. In the Guides section, use the pop-up menu to select another color. (In the illustration at right, Medium Blue was selected because the cyan-colored guides didn't show up well against the light blue sky.) Click OK to make the change and close the dialog box.

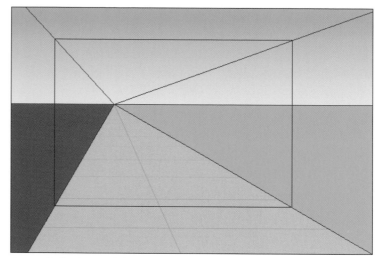

Create the background shapes

4   Create a new layer for objects that sit above the background shapes. Check the View menu and make sure that the Snap to Point option is turned on. Create and fill the shape for the front plane of the first object in your drawing. Draw a flat shape with no distortion. Deselect the shape.

5   Select the pen tool and draw a line from one of the corner points to the vanishing point. With the line still selected, choose View > Guides > Make Guides. Repeat this step for key points and angles on the front plane.

This example shows guides added to create the bottom, back, and right side of the box.

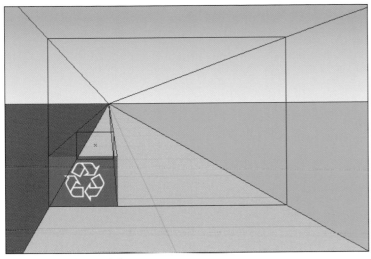

Create the background shapes

6 Draw the sides of the object using the guides. Paint the sides with colors that differ slightly from the front shape. Repeat steps 4 through 6 for each new object you create. Continue with the Perspective Transforming technique on page 124 to transform objects in perspective.

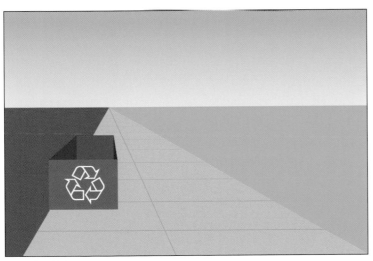

Completed object in perspective

Shortcut: Scale precisely

If you want to scale an object by a specific percentage, do this:

1 Select the scale tool in the toolbox.

2 Option/Alt-click to set the origin point of the scale. To make the origin point be the center of the selected object, double-click the scale tool in the toolbox.

3 Enter an amount in the Uniform or Non-Uniform option. Either click OK to scale the object or click Copy to scale the object and leave a copy of the original.

Perspective transforming

1 To create multiple shapes that recede toward the vanishing point, create the frontmost shape using the guidelines; then select the shape. Choose View and turn on Smart Guides. Choose Illustrator > Preferences > General (Mac OS X) or Edit > Preferences > General (Windows) and select the Scale Strokes & Effects option.

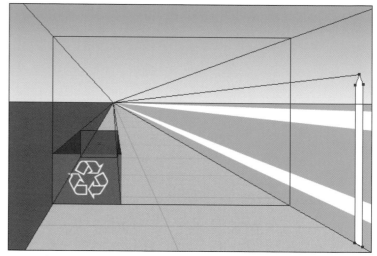

Create the frontmost shape

2 Select the scale tool, and then click the vanishing point once to set the origin point. Move the cursor to a point on the selected shape that intersects one of the guides. Drag the point along the guideline toward the vanishing point, and as you drag, press Option/Alt. Release the mouse button and then Option/Alt to make a copy.

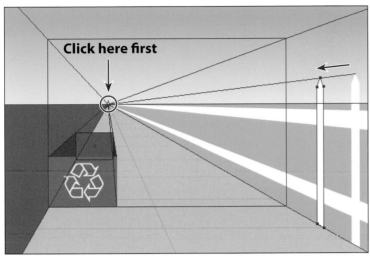

Scale and duplicate the shape

3 To make additional receding copies, choose Object > Transform > Transform Again (Command/Ctrl+D) for as many copies as you need.

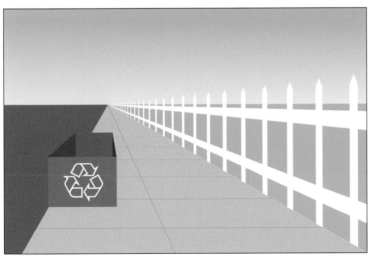

Final receding copies

Making color recede

Once you've created a set of transformed shapes that appear to recede into space, finish them by adding color that also recedes. Try this:

1 Follow the Perspective Transforming technique to create a set of shapes that are scaled in perspective.

2 Paint the frontmost object darker than the backmost object. Select the front and back objects, and all objects between them.

3 Choose Filter > Colors > Blend Front to Back. The filter blends the colors smoothly from the dark front to the lighter back shape. Repeat for other scaled shapes in the illustration.

Finessing stroke blends

Here's how to adjust the ends of strokes blended in perspective to the guide angles:

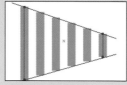

Blend with strokes

1 Before creating the blend, select the beginning and end stroke. Choose Object > Path > Outline Stroke.

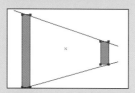

2 With the direct selection tool, select a corner point and Shift-drag it until the corner snaps to the guide. Repeat for each corner.

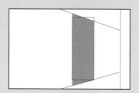

3 Shift-select both shapes and choose Object > Blend > Make to create the new blend.

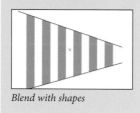

Blend with shapes

Perspective blending

1 To create evenly spaced lines or shapes on the sides of objects, draw the frontmost shape using the perspective guidelines.

In this example, drawing a shape—instead of stroking a line—ensured that the top and bottom of the line were angled properly. See "Finessing stroke blends" at the left for more information.

2 Use the scale tool as instructed in step 2 of the Perspective Transforming technique on page 124 to create a smaller copy of the line or shape at the far end of the surface.

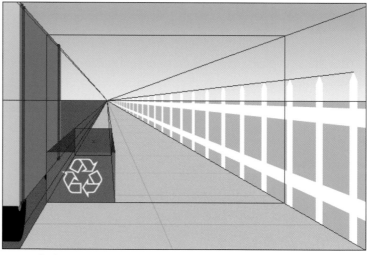

Create the beginning and end shapes for the blend

3 Select both lines or shapes, and choose Object > Blend > Make.

4 With the blend still selected, choose Object > Blend > Blend Options. Select Specified Steps for the Spacing and try different numbers of steps until you are satisfied with the effect. Click OK.

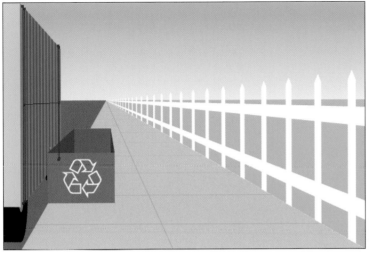

Create the blend

5 Add other objects to complete the illustration using the
guides, the vanishing point, and the horizon line as aides in
their construction.

Complete the illustration

19 | Foliage

Creating large areas of leaves, grass, and flowers is a snap with Illustrator's symbolism tools. You can make an endless number of fields with just one symbol. In this technique you'll create a group of grass blade shapes and define it as a symbol. (You can do this with other types of foliage, too.) After you create a symbol set, you'll customize it so that when you've finished, you'll have a field of randomly placed blades of grass—shaded, scaled, and colored—just as in nature. You can use more than one symbol in a symbol set. Try making several symbols with different sizes, shapes, and colors of grass.

Basic symbol set

1   Create several grass blade shapes with the pen tool. Paint them a few different colors of green. Spread them out so that you can see white space between them. Select the blades of grass with the selection tool.

2   Choose Window > Symbols to display the Symbols palette. Click the New Symbol button at the bottom of the palette to create a new symbol from the selected artwork. If you want to name the symbol, double-click the thumbnail and name it Tall Grass.

Create the symbol artwork

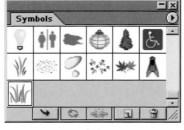
Create a new symbol

3   Choose Window > Layers to display the Layers palette. Create a new layer, and name it Grass Field. Hide the layer on which you created the symbol artwork.

4   Double-click the symbol sprayer tool in the toolbox to open the Symbolism Tools Options dialog box. Select a diameter

What can be in a symbol?

- Paths
- Compound paths
- Text
- Groups
- Raster images
- Embedded art and images
- Mesh objects
- Brush strokes
- Blends
- Symbol instances
- Effects

Mixing symbols

You can mix symbols in the same symbol set. Once you've used the symbol sprayer in step 5, you can select a different symbol and add that to the symbol set with the symbol sprayer. For example, you could add several types of grasses to one symbol set. Then, when you are ready to use the other symbolism tools on the symbol set, Shift-click to select each of the symbols in the Symbols palette that you want to be affected.

for the tool. This example used a diameter of 36 points because the illustration is small. Click OK.

Hide the original layer

Set Symbolism tool options

5 Use the symbol sprayer tool to create a small field of grass. As you press the mouse button and move the sprayer around the artwork, more blades of grass are created.

Use the symbol sprayer tool

6 Display the Color palette, and select a green fill color that is not part of the grass blade symbol art. You'll use this color in the next step to colorize the grass blades with the symbol stainer tool.

7   Select the symbol stainer tool in the toolbox. Gently paint over a few areas of the symbol set to change the colors of some of the grass blades.

Use the symbol stainer tool

8   Select the symbol sizer tool in the toolbox. Press Option/ Alt and click over a few areas of the symbol set to reduce the size of the grass blades. Use the tool without pressing Option/Alt to increase the size of the grass blades.

9   Select the symbol shifter tool in the toolbox. Drag over a few areas of the symbol set to move the blade symbols around. If you are satisfied with the artwork, save the file. If you want to add a style to parts of the symbol set, deselect the symbol set and continue with the next step.

Use the symbol sizer tool

About resolution and effects

Changing the resolution in the Document Raster Effects Settings dialog may change how the effects look. For example, a Gaussian blur of 1.0 pixels looks very pronounced at Screen resolution (72 ppi) but is barely noticeable at High resolution (300 ppi). Once you've changed your document resolution, go back and check all the effects and appearances. You may need to adjust some of them to accommodate the new resolution.

Shortcut: Change the symbolism tool diameter

To change the diameter of any symbolism tool as you use it, press the [(left bracket) key to decrease it and press the] (right bracket) key to increase it.

Use the symbol shifter tool

Symbol set with graphic style

1   To create a graphic style and then add it to the symbol set, make sure that nothing is selected. Choose Window > Appearance to display the Appearance palette. Depending on what object was selected last, the palette may contain a Stroke or Fill color. If so, click the Clear Appearance button at the bottom of the Appearance palette.

2   Choose Effect > Stylize > Drop Shadow to create a small shadow for the grass. Change the Opacity to 25%. Set the X and Y Offset value to 1 point. Set the Blur to 0 points and select the Color option. Change the color to a dark green by clicking the color swatch and choosing a color in the color picker. Click OK twice to apply the shadow to the appearance.

Clear the appearance   *Create a drop shadow*

3 Choose Window > Transparency to display the Transparency palette. Choose either Multiply or Screen for the blending mode. Multiply makes the grass blades darker where they overlap other blades. Screen makes the blades lighter where they overlap.

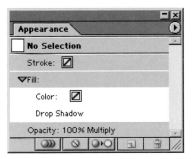

Complete the appearance

4 Display the Graphic Styles palette by choosing Window > Graphic Styles. Drag the Appearance thumbnail onto the Graphic Styles palette. Double-click the style thumbnail and name the new style Grass Shadow. Click OK.

5 Select the symbol set in the artwork. Select the Grass Shadow style in the Styles palette. Select the symbol styler tool in the toolbox and gently stroke across the areas where you want the grass blades shaded (or lightened ones if you used the Screen mode in step 3).

Use the symbol styler

Section 3 | Display type effects

Paula's Posies

Rock her world with roses! · Bowl him over with begonias! · Dazzle her with daisies!
Order now for Valentine's Day · 1.800.111.0000

Type masks are easy to create and edit, thanks to layers and grouping. How to save the type depends on the final destination of the image. If you plan to use the file for a Web graphic, you'll want to rasterize the type. If you'll print the file, you'll want to leave the type unrasterized. If you plan to share the file, you may want to convert the type to outlines to avoid problems if others don't have the proper fonts; but before converting the type, save the original file so that you can edit the type if needed. With any of these methods, heavy sans-serif typefaces usually make the best-looking masks.

1   Open or create a new file. Select the type tool, and create the type that will mask the image.

For optimal legibility of the type and image, use a large, bold typeface. A thin typeface design tends to lose its shape when filled with an image, and often the image within is unrecognizable.

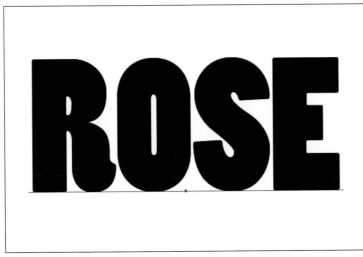

Create the type for the mask

2   Click the selection tool to select the type. Then choose Window > Info to display the Info palette. Make a note of the width and height of the type to use in step 3.

What typefaces work well as masks?

Best typeface designs for masks are:
- Sans serif
- Bold, heavy, or black styles
- Simple designs

What typefaces don't work well as masks?

For best results, don't use these typefaces for masks:
- Ornate script faces
- Light, thin, or condensed styles
- Highly stylized or illustrative designs
- Faces with delicate serifs

Viewing selected type without the highlight

Sometimes you aren't sure which typeface to use and need to try several before you decide. If you have selected your type, press Command/Ctrl+H to hide and show the text highlighting. Don't forget that the text is still selected before you go on to another task. Press Command/Ctrl+H again to show the highlighting.

These measurements will be helpful in determining the size your image needs to be. If it's too small, the type won't be completely filled.

Note the width and height

3   Switch to Photoshop and open the image you will mask with the type. Select the crop tool in the toolbox. Refer to the numbers you noted in step 2 and, in the Options bar, enter a Width and Height value that is almost a quarter larger than the width and height of the type. Enter whatever resolution you want.

Enter the crop tool parameters in Photoshop

4   Use the crop tool to select the area of the image that will be masked by type. Press Return/Enter to crop the image. Save the file.

It's a good idea to keep the image about 20% larger than the type. That way you'll have room to reposition the image within the type once it's masked.

5   Return to the Illustrator file and choose File > Place. Navigate to the Photoshop file you saved in step 4, and click Place. With the placed image still selected, choose Object > Arrange > Send to Back to move the image behind the type.

For the type to mask the image, it must be in front of the image.

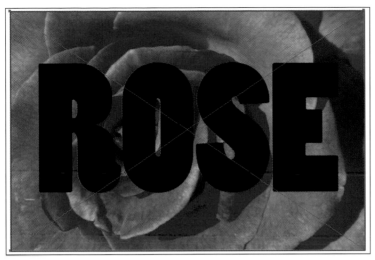

Place the image behind the type

6 Select both the type and the image, and choose Object > Clipping Mask > Make. If this file will be combined with other graphics, it's a good idea to group the type mask with the image. To group the two, select both the type and image, and choose Object > Group. Save the file.

The typeface or size can be changed at any time. To edit the type mask, use the type tool to select and change the type.

Create the clipping mask

21 | Multiple-outline type

You can create shapes with multiple outlines in Illustrator by using the Appearance palette to add strokes on top of each other and paint them with different colors and stroke weights. The top level in the Appearance palette is a color fill, which hides the half of the stroke that appears inside the path. Using this technique gives you the ability to edit the colors, line widths, and typeface easily. To use the appearance before you start with other images or on other objects, save it as a style. For help in determining line weights for the strokes, see "Layering strokes" on page 145.

Multi-outline type

1   Use the type tool to create the word or letters you want to outline.

For best results, avoid using script typefaces or specialty faces with inlines or other embellishments.

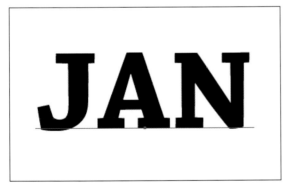

Create the type

2   Choose Window > Type > Character, and enter a positive number for the Tracking value.

The amount needed varies with each typeface and the thickness of the thickest stroke. You can adjust the tracking and type style in step 11, when you've finished stroking the type.

3   Choose Window > Appearance to display the Appearance palette. From the palette menu, choose Add New Fill.

Kerning vs. tracking

Because you are adding strokes to the outside edges of your type, you need to make more room between the letters.

Start by increasing the tracking value in step 2. Tracking adds a uniform amount of space between all the characters that are selected.

If you want to increase or decrease the space between two letters, use kerning values. You may want to make this adjustment at the end of the technique. To adjust the kerning value between two letters, click between the letters and enter a value in the Kerning text box.

Shortcut: Adjust kerning or tracking

To add or remove space between two characters, press Option/Alt+Right Arrow or Left Arrow.

To add or remove space between characters by 5 times the increment value, press Command/Ctrl+Option/ Alt+Right Arrow or Left Arrow.

To change the default tracking increment value of 20/1000 of an em, choose Illustrator > Preferences > Type & Auto Tracing (Mac OS X) or Edit > Preferences > Type & Auto Tracing (Windows). Then enter a new value in the Tracking text box.

Don't worry if the fill is the wrong color; you'll change that in the next step.

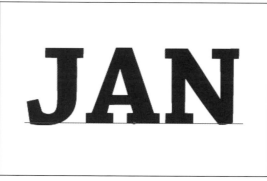

Increase the tracking value   *Add a new fill*

4   With the Fill item still selected in the Appearance palette, change the color in the Color palette, if desired.

Change the fill color

5   With the type still selected, choose Add New Stroke from the Appearance palette menu.

You'll change the color and stroke weight in step 7.

6   In the Appearance palette, drag the Stroke item down and place it beneath the Fill item.

The stacking order of strokes and fills directly affects an object's appearance. The Fill item should always be on top of the strokes to maintain the integrity of the original letterform. For more information, see "Stroked typefaces" on page 145.

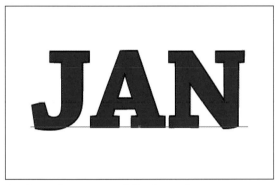

Add a new stroke   Drag the stroke below the fill

7 Evaluate the stroke weight and color. Change them if necessary. Remember that the stroke weight you use will effectively be cut in half in your illustration.

For example, this illustration used a 1-point black stroke; you see a 0.5-point stroke in the artwork because the top layer covers up the inner half of the stroke.

JAN

1-point stroke appears as 0.5-point stroke

8 With the type still selected, choose Add New Stroke from the Appearance palette menu. Move the stroke down below the first stroke you made in the Appearance palette. Change its color in the Color palette. Make the stroke weight larger than the first stroke you made.

Scaling an outlined typeface

To change the type size on an outlined typeface, you can either scale it with the scale tool or change it with the type tool. Each method gives different results. If you want to keep the multiple outlines the same but change the type size, select the type with the type tool and change the font size in the Character palette. If you want to change the type size and the lines together, use the scale tool. But first choose Illustrator > Preferences > General (Mac OS X) or Edit > Preferences > General (Windows), and select the Scale Strokes and Effects option. Then when you scale the type, the outlines will scale with it.

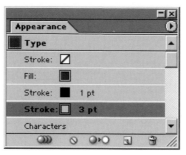

Add a new stroke

9   Repeat step 8 until you have as many strokes around the type as desired.

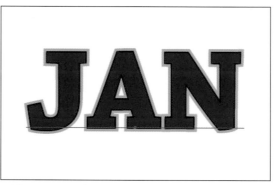

Add as many strokes as you desire

10 Click each Stroke item in the Appearance palette and in turn click the Round Join button in the Stroke palette.

Depending on the typeface design you choose, the outlines may display some odd-looking corners. Using a Round Join for the stroke corners will correct this problem.

11 While the type is still selected, adjust the tracking if necessary. You can also change the typeface and type size if desired.

Remember that if you change the type size, the stroke weights will not change; you may need to adjust them after resizing the type.

Use the Round Join option for each stroke

Stroked typefaces

Before you begin, here's how to determine the best stroke widths for your type outlines.

- When you stroke type, Illustrator creates the stroke from the center of the path that defines the outer edge of the letter. Thus, a stroke value of 6 points will create a 3-point border outside the edge and a 3-point border inside it.

- The stroke value of each consecutive layer determines the width of the border beneath it; for example, a 4-point stroke on top of a 6-point stroke will produce a border of 1 point (6/2 – 4/2).

- To figure out what stroke values to use before you start, draw a little sketch like the following one.

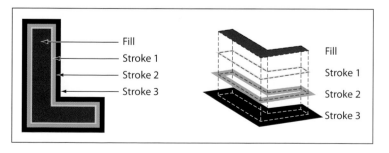

Layering strokes

When stroking type, it's important to use the Appearance palette to layer the fill above the stroke. Ordering the fill above the stroke maintains the integrity and beauty of the original design. Notice how the heavy stroke eats away at the letter-form in the letter that has the stroke above the fill.

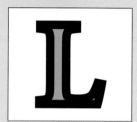

Stroke above the fill

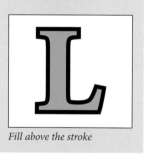

Fill above the stroke

...but the greatest of these is love.

Make your type look as if it were painted onto the page by a master calligrapher. Simply add a paintbrush stroke to the type in the Appearance palette. This method is the only way to add a brush stroke to type and keep it editable. Once you've completed this technique, you can still change the type style, size, and content with the type tool. Follow the variations if you want the type to have double, overlapping strokes or a roughened edge. You can also create just the outlines with brush strokes. Try different combinations of strokes to make your own effects.

1 Select the type tool in the toolbox. Click once and enter the type that you will make into paintbrush type.

The example below uses 135-point Brioso Pro Bold Display.

Create some text

2 With the type still selected, choose the selection tool in the toolbox. (If the type was not selected, select it with the selection tool.)

3 Choose Window > Appearance to display the Appearance palette. From the Appearance palette pop-up menu, choose Add New Stroke.

Using alternate characters

If you use an OpenType font for a painterly or calligraphic effect, try out some of that font's alternate characters. (Note: Warnock Pro and Brioso Pro are two OpenType fonts that may have come with your software.) The character sets of OpenType fonts vary. Here's how to view and turn on the available options.

1 Choose Window > Type > OpenType to display the palette.

Original

Original OpenType settings

2 Click the buttons at the bottom of the palette to use the font's alternate characters. (Dimmed buttons indicate unavailable options.)

Swash character used

Choosing a brush for predictable results

When choosing a brush to stroke type, remember that not all brushes paint with 100% of the stroke color. If you use a brush that appears gray in the palette, it will paint the brushstroke with less than 100% of the stroke color. The following examples show the same letter stroked with two different brushes. The middle example uses the Calligraphy 1 brush, which appears solid black in the palette. The bottom example uses the Calligraphy 2 brush, which appears gray in the palette.

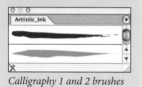

Calligraphy 1 and 2 brushes

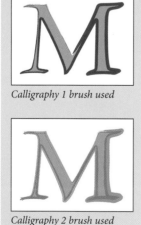

Calligraphy 1 brush used

Calligraphy 2 brush used

You can only add a brush stroke to type by first adding the stroke in the Appearance palette and then applying a brush (as in step 5). You cannot add brush strokes to type that was stroked using the Color palette.

4   Choose Window > Color to open the Color palette. Change the color of the stroke.

Add a stroke in the Appearance palette   Change the color of the stroke

5   Choose Window > Brushes to open the Brushes palette. From the pop-up menu, choose Open Brush Library > Artistic_ChalkCharcoalPencil. Select the Chalk-Scribble brush. (Choose List Views from the palette menu to display the brushes by name.)

Apply the Chalk-Scribble brush to the stroke

6 At the bottom of the Brushes palette, click the Options of Selected Object button. Change the Width size to better fit the type size you used. Depending on the effect you want, try either Flip option as well. When you are satisfied with the preview, click OK.

Change the size of the brush stroke

7 To change the fill color of the letters, click the Fill item in the Appearance palette. In the Color palette, choose a new fill color for the type.

8 To save the appearance as a style, drag the thumbnail at the top of the Appearance palette onto the Graphic Styles palette. The style will appear the same used on shapes or type. If you want to use this graphic style on other type, you must first outline the type (select the type and choose Type > Create Outlines). Then select the graphic style in the Graphic Styles palette.

Shortcut: Force the preview to update

Even though the preview option is selected in a dialog box, the preview doesn't always update after you've typed in the amount. This is because Illustrator doesn't understand that you've finished typing the number. To keep the dialog box open and force the number entry, press the Tab key. The focus will shift to the next entry field and the preview will update to reflect the change you just made—all this without closing the dialog box. Forcing the preview is handy because you may need to try several different values before you find the one you like.

Repainting a paint brush

Here's how to change a brush's fill color. (To change its stroke, see "Choosing a brush for predictable results" on page 148.)

1   Drag the brush from the palette onto the artboard. The brush artwork and its bounding box will appear.

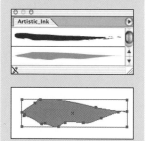

Drag brush onto the artboard

2   Using the direct selection tool, deselect the bounding box. Paint the brush artwork with a new color (here, 100% black).

3   With the artwork still selected, Shift-select the bounding box. Drag the selection onto the Brushes palette. In the New Brush dialog box, select New Art brush and click OK. Name the brush and Click OK. The new brush will appear in the Brushes palette.

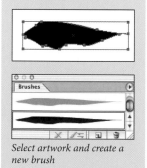

Select artwork and create a new brush

Change the fill color of the type characters

Variation: Double-stroke watercolor type

For a multicolored, multitextured watercolor effect, try adding two watercolor paintbrush strokes to the type. Here's how to do it.

1   Follow the Paintbrush Type technique. In step 5, open the Artistic_Watercolor brush library and choose the Watercolor Stroke 4 brush.

Use the Watercolor Stroke 4 brush

2 Select the type with the selection tool. In the Appearance palette, choose Add New Stroke to add a second stroke.

3 Choose Window > Color to open the Color palette. Change the color of the stroke.

4 In the Artistic_Watercolor brush library palette, choose Watercolor Stroke 2.

5 At the bottom of the Brushes palette, click the Options of Selected Object button. Change the Width size to better fit the type size you used. It may not necessarily be the same amount that you used on the first watercolor brush.

6 With the Watercolor Stroke 2 item still selected in the Appearance palette, choose Window > Transparency to display the Transparency palette. Choose Multiply from the Blending mode pop-up menu.

Rearranging the brushstrokes

To subtly vary the effects of multiple brushstrokes on type, change the order of the strokes in the Appearance palette. To do this, select the type with the selection tool. Then, in the Appearance palette, move one of the strokes above or below the other.

Original

Original appearance

Rearranged variation

New appearance order

Creating unfilled paintbrush type

If you want only the paint-brush around the edges of type with no fill, follow steps 1 through 6 of the Paintbrush Type technique. Then, in the Appearance palette, double-click the Characters item to select the type and the type tool. In the Color palette, choose None for the fill.

Original type

Completed paintbrush type

Unfilled paintbrush type

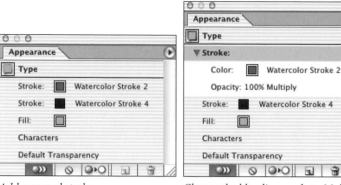

Add a second stroke *Change the blending mode to Multiply*

Variation: Rough-edged type

This technique simulates roughened edges on the typeface by adding a brush to the edges with the same color as the background.

1   Follow steps 1 through 3 of the Paintbrush Type technique. Use the Color palette to fill the type with a color.

Follow steps 1 through 3 of the Paintbrush Type technique

2 In step 4, use white for the color of the stroke. Or, if your background is a color other than white, use that color for the stroke.

3 In step 5, choose the Charcoal-Tapered brush from the Artistic_ChalkCharcoal Pencil brush library.

4 Continue with step 6 of the Paintbrush Type technique.

Use the Charcoal Tapered brush painted with the background color (white)

Creating a spattered ink look

Several brushes give a spattered ink effect. You can apply the effect by using the paintbrush tool and painting spatters wherever you want them. Or you can add the spatters to the type in the Appearance palette.

To get the look of the following samples, follow the Double-stroke Watercolor Type variation. For the first stroke, use the Fountain Pen brush in the Artistic_Ink brush library. For the second stroke, use the Ink Spatter 1 brush in the Artistic_Ink brush library.

Fountain Pen brush stroke

Completed ink-spattered type

23 Corroded type

Some designers try to simulate an eroded or weathered type effect by making a series of photocopies in which each copy is made from the previous copy. The following technique lets you achieve a similar look with more control and less wasted paper. The technique produces a typeface with small holes in it and corroded edges.

Eroded type

1   Create some type. The following example uses 130-point Adobe Caslon Pro Bold.

Create some type

2   With the type still selected, use the Color palette and change the fill to None.

You need to remove the fill now so that it won't cover up the Scribble effect you will add in step 6. Even though the type is invisible, it is still there.

3   Choose Window > Appearance to display the Appearance palette. Double-click the words "Type: No Appearance" in the palette to select the type as an object and switch to the selection tool. From the Appearance palette menu, choose Add New Fill.

4   In the Color palette, change the fill color to whatever color you like.

5 In the Appearance palette, make sure that the Fill item is selected.

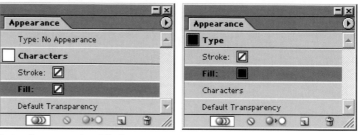

Paint the type with a fill of None   *Select the Fill item*

6 Choose Effect > Stylize > Scribble to open the Scribble Options dialog box. Turn on the Preview option. Start with the settings in the following illustration. Adjust them as needed for your particular typeface. Click OK.

Apply the Scribble effect to the fill

First layer of the Scribble effect

7   If you like the effect, save the file. If you want a more randomly corroded effect, continue with this step. From the Appearance palette menu, choose Add New Fill. The new fill will cover up the Scribble effect from the first fill. Paint the fill the same color as the first fill.

8   Choose Effect > Stylize > Scribble. Turn on the Preview option. Use the following settings. Angle = –98°; Path Overlap = –2 with Variation = 0.8; Stroke Width = 0.5; Curviness = 3 with Variation = 2; and Spacing = 1.5 with Variation = 0.9. Click OK when you are satisfied with the look.

Two layers of the Scribble effect

Adjusting the path overlap

When using the Scribble effect with type, adjust the path overlap to maintain or erode the edges of the letterforms. Shown here, the red outline is the original letterform; the blue Scribble effects reflect different Path Overlap values.

Path Overlap = 0, Variation = 0

Path Overlap = 3.5, Variation = 0

Path Overlap = –3.5, Variation = 0

Path Overlap = –3.5, Variation=4.5

9 If you like the effect, save the file. If you want even more of a corroded effect, add another fill by choosing Add New Fill from the Appearance palette menu. Paint the fill the same color as the first and second fills.

10 With the Fill item still selected, choose Effect > Stylize > Scribble. Turn on the Preview option. Use the following settings: Angle = 106°; Path Overlap = –0.75 with Variation = 0.8; Stroke Width = 0.5; Curviness = 0 with Variation = 0; and Spacing = 0.8 with Variation = 0.9. Click OK when you are satisfied with the look.

Three layers of the Scribble effect

11 To increase the roughness of the edges or add more little "holes," change the Scribble effect settings by double-clicking any of the Scribble items in the Appearance palette. Make the adjustment and click OK. In the following example, the spacing was increased and the stroke width was decreased to create more white holes.

Final eroded type

Corroded type graphic style

1   With the type object selected, choose New Graphic Style from the Graphic Styles palette menu. Name the style and click OK.

2   Apply the style you created to layers or individual paths. You can also change the style's colors or stroke weights to create a new style.

In this example, the corroded style was applied to the type and graphics, and then the colors for each fill were changed in the Appearance palette.

Graphic style applied to artwork and fill colors changed

Scratchboard is a kind of illustration board that is specially made with a black surface and an underlying white surface. The dark surface is scratched away to reveal the image in white. In this technique you will create type with one or more layers of "scratching" using the Scribble effect. You can use the Crosshatch Scratchboard Type technique to get several layers of scratching that overlap each other at different angles. Or you can use the Woodcut Scratchboard Type technique to get a rough, uneven carved look.

Crosshatch scratchboard type

1   Create a background shape and paint it black.

2   Create some type, graphics, or both, and paint them white to give you an idea of how the color will look.

This example shows white type and a graphic that is from a picture typeface.

Create a black background with white type

3   With the type still selected, use the Color palette and change the fill to None. (The stroke should also be set to None.)

Maintaining the typeface shape

If you want to maintain the crosshatched type's shape, try adding a stroke in the Appearance palette. To do this, simply select the type and choose Add New Stroke from the Appearance palette menu. If you want the stroke barely visible, use a .25-point stroke width and paint it the same color as the cross-hatching.

Add a small stroke to maintain the form

You need to remove the white fill now so that it won't cover up the Scribble effect that you will add in step 7. Even though the type is invisible, it is still there.

4   Choose Window > Appearance to display the Appearance palette. Double-click the words "Type: No Appearance" in the palette to select the type as an object and switch to the selection tool. From the Appearance palette menu, choose Add New Fill.

5   In the Color palette, change the fill to white.

Even though it is a fill, this white color will define the scribble strokes you will add in step 7.

6   In the Appearance palette, make sure that the Fill item is selected.

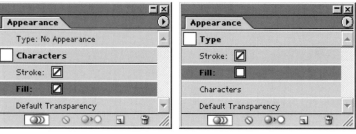

Paint the type with a fill of None   *Select the Fill item*

7   Choose Effect > Stylize > Scribble to open the Scribble dialog box. Turn on the Preview option. Start with the settings in the following illustration. Adjust them as needed for your particular typeface. Click OK when you are satisfied with the look for the first layer of scratching.

Scribble Options

Settings: Custom

Angle: 135 °

Path Overlap: -1.5 pt   Variation: 0.5 pt

Inside   Centered   Outside   None   Wide

Line Options

Stroke Width: 0.3 pt

Curviness: 4 %   Variation: 1 %

Angular   Loopy   None   Wide

Spacing: 5 pt   Variation: 5 pt

Tight   Loose   None   Wide

OK

Cancel

☑ Preview

Apply the Scribble effect to the white fill

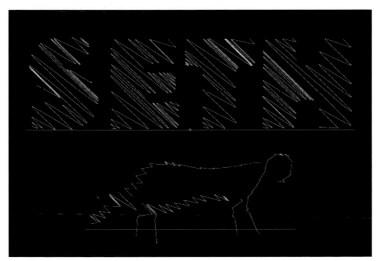

The first layer of scratching

8 From the Appearance palette menu, choose Add New Fill.
The new fill will cover up the Scribble effect from the first
fill. If the fill is not already white, paint it white.

Choosing the right settings for your typeface

Try to match the style of
crosshatch to the style and
attitude of your typeface. For
example, the top illustration
shown here uses a fun, casual
typeface. The loose, scattered
style of scribble goes well
with the type design. To make
the style loose, increase the
Spacing and Path Overlap
values and their variation
amounts.

The bottom example uses
a traditional serif typeface. To
maintain the letterform and
match the typeface design
better, tighten up the Scribble
effects. To make the style
tighter, decrease the Spacing
and Path Overlap values and
their variation amounts.
The bottom example also
uses a hairline stroke width
(.25-point) for a delicate
appearance.

*Looser scribbles for a casual
typeface*

*Tighter scribbles for a more
formal typeface*

9 Choose Effect > Stylize > Scribble. Turn on the Preview option. Use the same settings as in step 7, except change the angle to 45°. Click OK when you are satisfied with the look.

Two layers of scratching

10 Repeat steps 8 and 9 for the third layer of scratching, except use 0° for the angle.

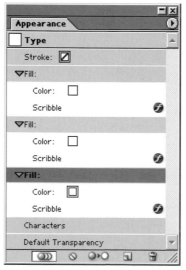

Add the third layer of scribbled fill

Three layers of scratching

Creating colored crosshatch scratches

To create a colored crosshatch effect, follow the Crosshatch Scratchboard Type technique. Instead of making the fill colors white, use a different color for each one.

Three-colored crosshatch

11 If you want to adjust the settings for the Scribble effect, double-click any of the Scribble items in the Appearance palette. Make the adjustment and click OK. In the following example, the spacing and path overlap were changed.

Final scratchboard illustration

Increasing the "scratchiness" of the type

If you want the scratches to look less linear and more broken up, try this:

1 Follow the Crosshatch Scratchboard Type technique.

2 In the Appearance palette, expand the display of one of the Fill items by clicking the arrow to its left.

3 Select the Color item and change the color to black (or whatever your background color is).

The bottom example has two of its three Fill items painted black.

Three white fill layers

Two black fill layers and one white fill layer

Woodcut scratchboard type

1 Follow steps 1 through 7 of the Crosshatch Scratchboard Type technique. In step 7, use the settings shown here.

Apply the Scribble effect to the white fill

2 With the type still selected, choose Object > Expand Appearance to turn the Scribble effect into a group of stroked paths.

3 To turn the paths into filled shapes, choose Object > Path > Outline Stroke. Choose View > Hide Edges to hide the selection edges and points so that you can view the effect in the next step.

Expand the appearance and outline the paths

4   To roughen up the shapes, choose Effect > Distort &
Transform > Twist. Turn on the Preview option. Use a value
between 0° and 4° depending on the effect you want. Click
OK when you are satisfied with the effect.

Apply the Twist effect

1960s poster type

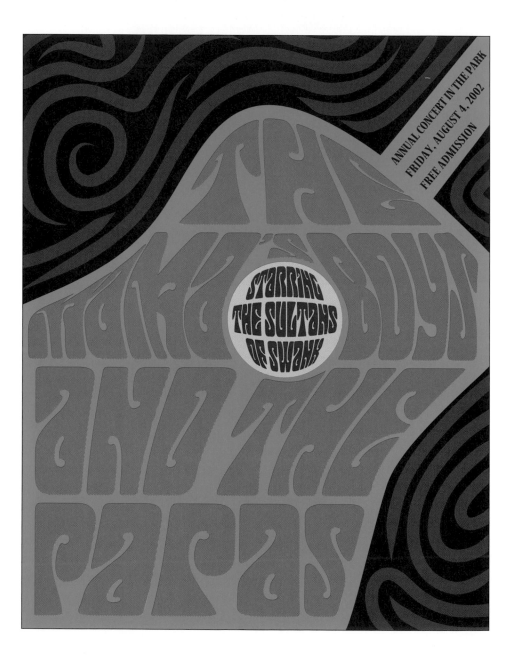

Many of the posters from the 1960s and '70s had hand-drawn typefaces that flowed into curved shapes. The posters were reminiscent of the Art Nouveau posters from the late 1800s. Inspired by flowers, leaves, and vines, the '60s poster artists created sinuous shapes that encapsulated the type. With Illustrator's Envelope feature, you can create type just as they did in the '60s. First you create the basic shape and divide it into type containers. Then you create the type and combine it with the shape to distort it. Choose your typeface carefully. The ones that work best are very fat, dense display faces.

Shortcut: Copy a layer
Duplicate a layer quickly by dragging its thumbnail onto the New Layer button at the bottom of the Layers palette. Change the name by double-clicking the layer name and typing a new name in the Layer Options dialog. Click OK to complete the change.

1   In a new Illustrator file or on a new layer, create the basic shape that will contain all of your type.

Keep the shape as simple as possible. The more intricate and complicated the shape, the less predictable (and satisfactory) the type distortion will be.

2   In the Layers palette, name the layer that contains the shape Type Background. Choose Duplicate "Type Background" from the Layers palette menu. Rename the new layer Type Shapes. Hide the Type Background layer.

Create a simple shape

What can you use envelopes with?

- Paths
- Patterns
- Gradients
- Raster images
- Embedded art and images
- Mesh objects
- Brush strokes
- Blends
- Symbol instances
- Effects
- Masks

If you use an envelope on a pattern-filled shape, the pattern won't distort unless you set the envelope options. Choose Object > Envelope Distort > Envelope Options. Select the Distort Pattern Fills option and click OK.

Create the Type Shapes layer

3 Using the pen tool, create lines that define where the type shapes will separate. Paint the lines with a stroke weight that's the width of space that you want between each type shape.

In this example, the lines are 2-point strokes because the desired separation between the type blocks is 2 points.

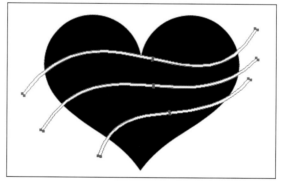

Create paths where the shapes will separate

4 Select all of the lines you created in step 3, and choose Object > Path > Outline Stroke. The lines have now become shapes. This will help when you create the separate type shapes in step 5.

If you want a backup file in case your type doesn't fit nicely and you need to change these lines, choose File > Save a Copy and save a backup version of the artwork at this stage.

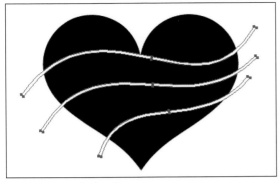

Outline the stroked paths

5 Display the Pathfinder palette. With the selection tool, Shift-select the lines you just outlined and the basic shape. Option/Alt-click the Subtract button in the Pathfinder palette to subtract the lines from the basic shape at the same time you expand the lines into regular objects. While the artwork is still selected, choose Object > Ungroup. Deselect the art.

Use pathfinder to separate the main shape into smaller shapes

6 Use the type tool to create one type object for each shape. Choose a heavy, thick typeface. Plan the text according to the size of the shape that will hold the text.

For example, the two top shapes in the heart will contain small text blocks, while the two middle shapes will contain longer words or phrases.

Fitting type in an envelope

When adjusting the type to fit, try changing the Fidelity percentage. This determines how closely the object fits the envelope mold. It may increase the preview time slightly, but it may also make the type look better. Choose Object > Envelope Distort > Envelope Options. Set the Fidelity percentage higher for a tighter fit and lower for a looser fit.

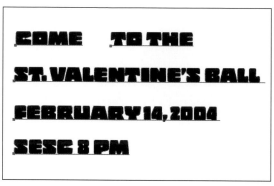

Create a type object for each shape

7 With the type still selected, choose Object > Arrange > Send to Back. Deselect the type.

8 Select one of the shapes, and then Shift-select the type object that will fit into it.

Shift-select the type and the shape

9 Choose Object > Envelope Distort > Make with Top Object.

Use Envelope Distort to create the first text object

10 Repeat steps 8 and 9 for each type object in your artwork. If you are satisfied with the effect, skip to step 13. If you want to edit or change the type, continue with the next step.

If you want to edit the dividing lines and you saved a copy of the file at step 4, open that file; edit the lines and start again at step 5.

Evaluate the type flow

11 If you want to edit the text or change the typeface, select the envelope object that needs editing. Choose Object > Envelope Distort > Edit Contents. To view the type more easily, choose View > Outline. Select the type tool in the toolbox and make the type changes.

Changing the envelope shape

To edit the envelope shape, select the envelope and choose Object > Envelope Distort > Edit Envelope. (It doesn't matter whether the envelope was made from a mesh or a warp.) To edit the shape, do one of the following:

- Use the direct selection tool to move any of the envelope's points. You can also select the points and delete them or adjust their direction lines.
- Use the mesh tool to add, delete, or edit points.
- Choose Object > Envelope Distort > Reset with Mesh or Reset with Warp. Click the Preview button to view the changes before you click OK.

Edit the type as needed

12 Choose View > Preview. If you are satisfied with the type changes, choose Object > Envelope Distort > Edit Envelope.

Preview the changes

13 If you want to change the color of the type, select the envelopes and choose Object > Envelope Distort > Edit Contents. Use the Color palette to select a new fill color. Deselect the type.

Add color to the type

14 To complete the effect, in the Layers palette show the Type Background layer. Select the original shape and paint it with a fill color. If you want the shape to appear slightly larger than the type, add a stroke to the shape that is the same color as its fill. Deselect and save the file.

Display the background shape

There are two ways to make headlines. One way requires becoming a celebrity and doing something controversial. The other way is to use Illustrator to create text that demands attention. Since the former is beyond the scope of this book, you'll focus on the latter. As you'll see, Illustrator has features like 3D and Warp to help create spectacular text headlines.

1   Select the type tool and click the artboard once. Type the word or words for your headline. Bold fonts with tight kerning work best. Switch to the selection tool to better view the changes in the next steps.

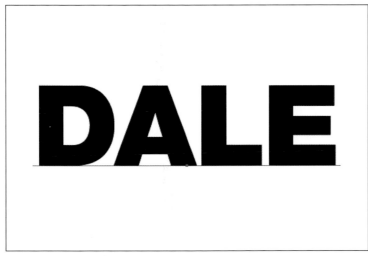

Create some big, bold type

2   Use the Color palette to select a fill color for your text. Then apply a stroke color. In the Stroke palette, set the stroke width to 0.25 point.

You're applying a stroke here because when you apply the 3D effect in step 4, you want the extrusion color to differ from the fill color.

Extruding with or without a stroke

Illustrator's 3D effect always uses the stroke color as the extrusion color. If no stroke is applied, Illustrator uses the fill color as the extrusion color.

Shape with fill and no stroke

Extruded shape with fill and no stroke

Shape with a fill and a stroke

Extruded shape with a fill and a stroke

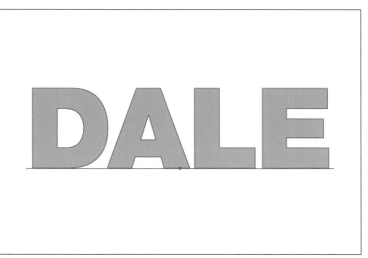

Paint the type with a fill and stroke

3   Choose Effect > Warp > Arch. (Be sure to choose Arch, not Arc.) Turn on the Preview option. Choose a subtle Bend value of 15%. For distortion, set the Horizontal value to −25%. This gives the appearance that the text is fading into the distance, and will be exaggerated slightly once the 3D effect is applied. Click OK.

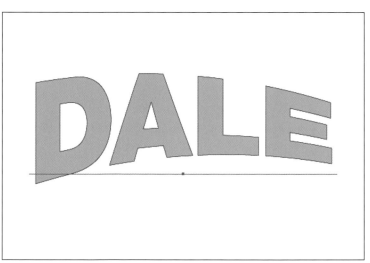

Apply a Warp effect

4 With the type object still selected, choose Effect > 3D > Extrude & Bevel. Turn on the Preview option. The default Off-Axis Front view is well-suited for this task. Depending on your use of the headline, you may also want to adjust the Extrude Depth amount. Set the Perspective to 50°, which gives the text a drop of urgency.

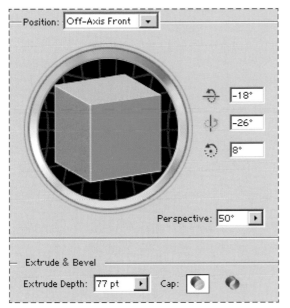

Adjust the extrude depth and add some perspective

5 Click More options. Choose No Shading from the Surface pop-up menu near the bottom of the 3D Extrude & Bevel Options dialog box. For headlines, you want to keep the vibrant colors that you applied to the text. The strong colors also make the extrusion appear contiguous and consistent. Click OK.

Stroking 3D objects

It's important to know how a stroke affects a 3D object because certain features act differently when a stroke is applied. For example, when mapping artwork, a simple box with just a fill and no stroke will have 6 sides. But that same box with a stroke will have 24 sides when you try to map art to it, because the 3D effect sees the strokes as surfaces.

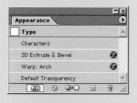

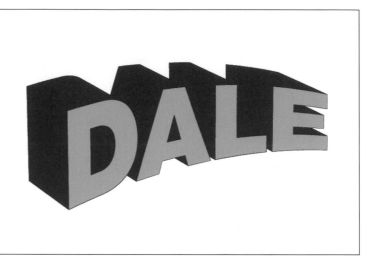

Paint the type with a fill and stroke

6 Define this headline look as a graphic style. Open the Graphic Styles palette (Window > Graphic Styles), and with the text object selected, Option/Alt-click the New Graphic Style button at the bottom of the palette, name your style (here, Superhero Type), and click OK. Notice that the thumbnail appears blank for the text-effect graphic style.

Chances are you'll want to use this look for other headlines. Rather than repeating all of these steps again (even if it's fun), you can reuse the look by defining it as a graphic style.

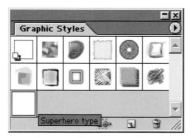

Save the text effect as a graphic style

Variation: Larger initial cap

1   Choose View > Outline (Command/Ctrl+Y) to edit the type more easily without the display of 3D effects. Select the first letter of your headline.

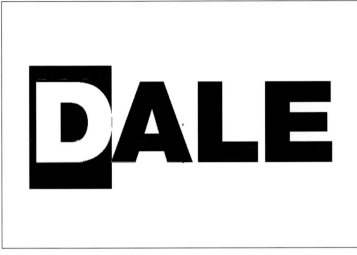

Switch to Outline view to edit type

2   Return to Preview view (Command/Ctrl+Y) and hide the selection edges (View > Hide Edges). Increase the point size in the Character palette to your satisfaction. Redisplay the selection edges (Command/Ctrl+H) and deselect.

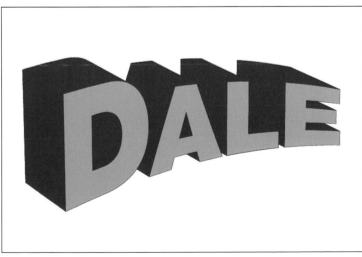

Increase the point size of the initial cap

27 | Beveled and embossed type

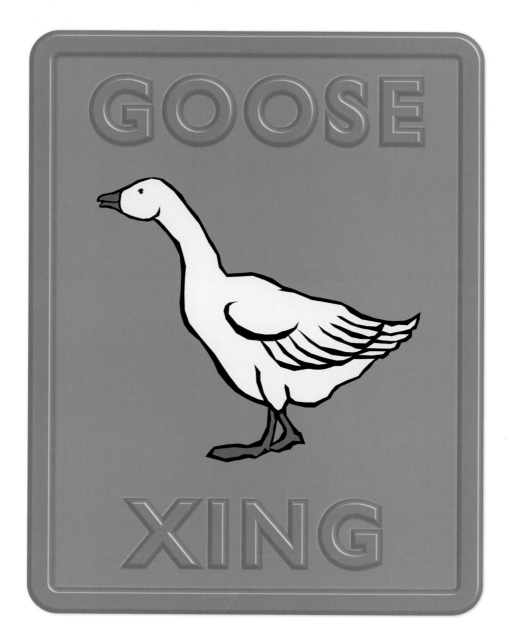

Three-dimensional type doesn't always have to be "superhero" block letters. It can also be subtly raised off the surface of the page. Or it can look as if it were embossed onto a background surface. With the following techniques, you can make your type look like slightly dimensional letters with chiseled edges; or you can go a little farther and add small shadows and highlights to create an embossed effect.

Beveled type

1   Select the type tool in the toolbox. Click once and enter the type that will become beveled type.

The following example uses 100-point Myriad Pro Bold.

2   With the type still selected, use the Color palette to select the color for the face of the letterforms.

Create some text and paint it

Choosing a typeface for bevelling

Pick a typeface for beveled or embossed type that's simple—neither too ornate nor condensed. These examples of beveled type show two that work well (top two) and two that don't (bottom two). The Edwardian Script typeface is too complex (note the self-intersecting bevels) and the Lo-Type too compact.

Minion Pro Italic

Warnock Pro Display

Edwardian Script ITC

Lo-Type Medium Condensed

Softening sharp corners

Beveling a shape with sharp corners or acute angles can produce unexpected and undesirable results. To get a more realistic embossed look, you may also want to soften the corners. Here's a way to tackle both problems without having to choose a different typeface.

1 Follow steps 1 and 2 of the Beveled Type technique.

2 Select the type with the selection tool and choose Type > Create Outlines.

3 Choose Filter > Stylize > Round Corners. Enter a value for the corner radius (1 point in the following example). Click OK.

4 Continue with step 3 of the Beveled Type technique.

Type with unrounded corners

Type with rounded corners

3 Select the type with the selection tool and choose Effect > 3D > Extrude & Bevel. Click More Options to display all the options. Start with the following settings, turn on the Preview option, and then adjust for your artwork. These setting work well for the typeface and size shown here. Your type may require slightly different settings.

Position: Front
Extrude Depth: 19 point
Cap: On (for solid appearance)
Bevel: Rounded
Height: 3 point
Bevel Extent Out
Surface: Plastic Shading
Light Intensity = 100%
Ambient Light = 75%
Highlight Intensity = 80%
Highlight Size = 90%
Blend Steps = 25

4 So that the light source matches the following example, move the light source to the upper left by dragging the square highlight within the circle. Adjust the settings for your typeface and size. When you are satisfied with the results, click OK.

3D Extrude & Bevel Options

Position: Front

OK

Cancel

Map Art...

Fewer Options

☑ Preview

⚠
Bevel self-intersection
may have occurred.

0°
0°
0°

Perspective: 0°

Extrude & Bevel

Extrude Depth: 19 pt   Cap:

Bevel: Rounded

Height: 3 pt

Surface: Plastic Shading

Light Intensity: 100%
Ambient Light: 75%
Highlight Intensity: 80%
Highlight Size: 90%
Blend Steps: 25

Shading Color: Black

☐ Preserve Spot Colors   ☐ Draw Hidden Faces

Apply the 3D Extrude & Bevel effect

5 Save the file. If you want to add a drop shadow and
highlight to the type to create an embossed effect, continue
with the Embossed Type technique.

Correcting self-intersecting bevels

Occasionally the 3D Extrude & Bevel Options dialog box displays the warning, "Bevel self-intersection may have occurred." What does this mean? Here are examples of beveled angles with self-intersecting and normal bevels.

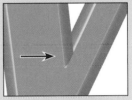

Type with self intersecting bevel

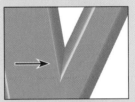

Type with normal bevel

Correcting the problem of self-intersection requires trial and error; it all depends on the type design, the height of the bevel, and the bevel design. Try one of the following ideas:

• Change typefaces.
• Follow the steps in "Softening sharp corners" on page 184.
• Reduce the height of the bevel.
• Increase the type size.

Scaling beveled type

Once you've created beveled type, you can scale it two different ways—each for a different result. To scale the bevel effect along with the type, choose Illustrator > Preferences > General (Mac OS X) or Edit > Preferences > General (Windows) and turn on the Scale Strokes & Effects option. Then use the scale tool to change the type size.

If you want the bevel effect to remain the same, use the Character palette to change the type size. This method works no matter what the preferences settings.

Original artwork

Scaled with the scale tool

Scaled with the Character palette

Completed beveled type

Embossed type

To create an embossed look for your beveled type, you will create a small, soft shadow and highlight. You will create the shadow first with a Drop Shadow effect. Then you'll duplicate the drop shadow and invert it so that it becomes a light glow instead of a dark shadow. This highlight will be positioned on the opposite side of the letterforms from the shadow.

1   Follow the Beveled Type technique.

2   Create a shape over the type that will be the background for the embossed type. Using the Color palette, fill the background shape with the same color as the type.

The type will no longer be visible because the shape is now in front of it.

3   With the shape still selected, choose Window > Layers to view the Layers palette. Double-click the name of the selected shape (<Path>) and rename it Background. Drag the Background path below the type path in the Layers palette. Lock the Background path in the Layers palette to avoid accidentally selecting the background as you work with the type.

The type should now be visible above the background shape.

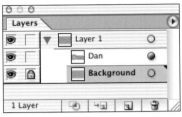

Move the background below the type

4   Use the selection tool to select the type and choose Effect >
    Stylize > Drop Shadow. Start with the following settings
    and turn on the Preview option. Adjust the settings for your
    typeface and size. When you are satisfied with the effect,
    click OK.

Apply the Drop Shadow effect

5   Make any final changes to the text. In the next series of
    steps, you will create a highlight that will be a separate
    image from the type. You will not be able to change the
    highlight's typeface or size or the content.

Type with drop shadow

6 In the Layers palette, duplicate the type by dragging its layer onto the New Layer button at the bottom of the palette.

7 Select the lower copy of the type in the Layers palette by clicking to the right of its target circle.

8 Choose Object > Expand Appearance to expand the drop shadow and 3D effects of the type.

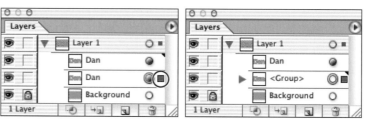

Duplicate and select the type   *Expand the appearance of the type*

9 Choose Select > Deselect. In the Layers palette, click the triangle to the left of the <Group> path to reveal its contents. Hide the <Group> sublayer by clicking its eye icon to the left, and select the <Image> sublayer by clicking to the right of its target circle.

10 Choose Window > Transparency to display the Transparency palette. Change the blend mode to Screen. Leave the Opacity setting as is.

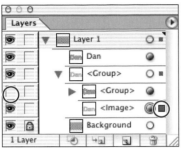

Select the drop shadow image and hide the type

Change the blend mode to Screen

11 With the <Image> sublayer selected, choose Filter > Colors > Invert Colors.

This changes the black drop shadow to a white drop shadow.

12 With the <Image> sublayer still selected, press the Up Arrow key two times. Then press the Left Arrow key two times to move the white highlight in the opposite direction from the drop shadow.

Move the highlight up and to the left

Section 4 Typography

28 | Circular type

C is for cat,

CHICKEN, COW, COUGAR, CRAB, CAMEL, CRICKET, CATERPILLAR, COLT, COBRA, COCKATOO AND COYOTE

Illustrator does a wonderful job of setting type around a circle. But sometimes you want the type on the bottom of the circle to be positioned right side up instead of upside down. And sometimes you want the type to bend and stretch with the curve. Here's how to create type around a circle so that the type is always right side up. It also leaves the type undistorted.

1 Create a new layer and name it Upper Type. Select the ellipse tool, press Shift, and create a circle that defines the inside baseline of your type. The stroke size doesn't matter because it will disappear once you create the text.

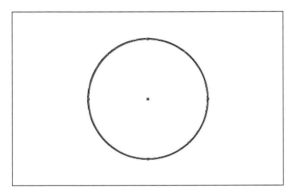

Create a circle

2 Select the path type tool and click the bottom anchor point of the circle. Enter only the text that you want to appear at the top of the circle. It may seem confusing that you start the text at the bottom of the circle but once you center the text, it moves to the top. You will enter the text for the bottom of the circle in a later step.

All caps work better than upper- and lowercase letters because no ascenders or descenders bisect the arc formed by the letters.

Shortcut: Change type alignment

Change the alignment of selected text with these keyboard shortcuts:
- Align paragraph left, right, or center:
    Command/Ctrl+Shift+L, R, or C
- Justify paragraph:
    Command/Ctrl+Shift+J

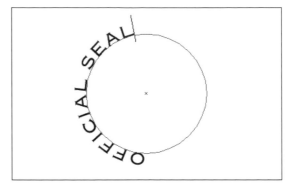

Add type along the circle path

3 Choose Select > All to select the type you just entered. Choose Window > Type > Paragraph to display the Paragraph palette. Click the Align Center button to center the type across the top of the circle.

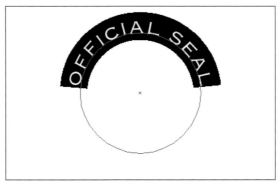

Change the paragraph alignment to center the type

4 Option/Alt-click the New Layer button at the bottom of the Layers palette. Name the new layer Lower Type and click OK.

5 With the type still selected, notice the selection indicator at the far right of the Upper Type layer in the Layers palette. Option/Alt-drag the selection indicator up to the Lower Type layer name in the Layers palette. This makes a copy of the type and places it on the Lower Type layer. Lock the Upper Type layer.

Create the Lower Type layer

Duplicate the type onto the Lower Type layer

6 Choose Type > Type on a Path > Type on a Path Options. Turn on the Preview option. Select the Flip option and choose Ascender from the Align to Path pop-up menu. Click OK.

Don't worry if the type is in the wrong position; you will adjust it in a later step.

Change the path type options

7 Select the path type tool, and choose Select > All to select the type you just duplicated. Replace the type with the new text that you want to appear on the bottom half of the circle.

Don't worry if the type overlaps the upper type; you will adjust this in the next step.

Rotating type around a circle

It can be difficult at times to control the brackets around the type on a path. If you simply want to rotate the type around a circle, try this:

1 Use the selection tool to select the type you want to rotate. You can also select it in the Layers palette by clicking to the far right of its path name.

2 Select the rotate tool in the toolbox. Drag the type in the direction you want it to rotate. When the preview is positioned properly, release the mouse button.

Completed rotation

Enter the type that will appear at the bottom of the circle

8 Choose the selection tool in the toolbox. You will now see the path and the brackets that define the beginning, center, and end of the type on a path. Because this is a circle, the brackets are stacked on top of each other. Move the pointer toward the brackets until the left arrow indicator is visible. Click and drag the bracket clockwise around the circle until the right and center brackets also are clearly visible. Move the brackets until you are satisfied with the position of the type on the circle. For another way to do this, see "Rotating type around a circle" on the left.

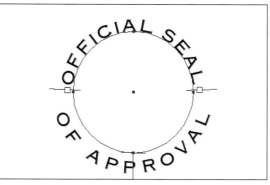

Move the brackets to position the type on the circle

9 With the type on a path still selected, choose View > Type > Character to display the Character palette, and then choose Show Options from the palette menu. Click the Baseline

Shift buttons in the Character palette to move the type so that the tops of the letters touch the edge of the circle.

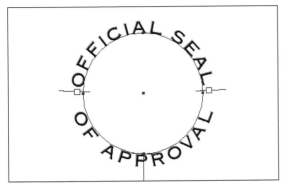

Adjust the baseline shift to fit the type to the circle

10 Depending on the type size and design, enter a fractional Baseline Shift amount if necessary. This example has a baseline shift of 6 points.

Change the Baseline Shift amount

11 In the Layers palette, unlock the Upper Type layer. With the selection tool, select both circles with their type. Adjust the tracking amount in the Character palette to fit the letters around the circle.

In this example, the tracking was set to 40.

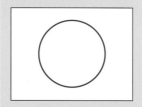

12 Readjust the position of the type on the circle if needed. Use the selection tool to drag the bracket. In this example, the space between the two *L*s was awkward, so it was reduced slightly.

Adjust the tracking and move the brackets if necessary

13 To add a border, select the ellipse tool. Position the tool over the center point of the type circles. Option/Alt-drag from the center point outward. Press Shift to constrain the object to a circle. Release the mouse button and then the Shift+Option/Alt keys. Repeat this step for as many borders as you want.

Add a border

Circular type positioning

The Circular Type technique shows how to position the type so that it is all right-reading. To make type simply wrap all the way around the circle path, here are just a few of your positioning options. Follow these steps:

1   Create a circle with the ellipse tool.
2   Select the path type tool and click the circle where you want the type to begin. Enter the text.
3   Choose the selection tool in the toolbox. Choose Type > Type on a Path > Type on a Path Options. Select one of the following settings:

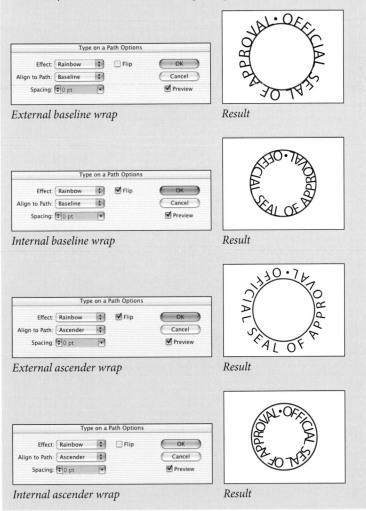

External baseline wrap   *Result*

Internal baseline wrap   *Result*

External ascender wrap   *Result*

Internal ascender wrap   *Result*

wo households, both alike in dignity,

In fair Verona, where we lay our scene,

From ancient grudge break to new mutiny,

Where civil blood makes civil hands unclean.

From forth the fatal loins of these two foes

A pair of star-cross'd lovers take their life;

Whole misadventured piteous overthrows

Do with their death bury their parents' strife.

The fearful passage of their death-mark'd love,

And the continuance of their parents' rage,

Which, but their children's end, nought could remove,

Is now the two hours' traffic of our stage;

The which if you with patient ears attend,

What here shall miss, our toil shall strive to mend.

From *Romeo and Juliet* by William Shakespeare

The initial cap represents a design technique that has withstood the test of time. Sometimes called a drop cap, this element has been used for centuries to emphasize the beginning of a chapter in a book, or the start of an article in a newspaper or magazine. Using Illustrator's text-wrap feature, it will take mere minutes to get your opening paragraph started in style.

Rectangular text wrap

1   Select the type tool and drag a text box to define the bounding area of the type. Alternatively, draw a closed path using any Illustrator drawing tool, and then click the path with the type tool to convert it to the bounding area.

2   Fill the bounding area with type. Use any of these techniques: Enter text directly by typing; paste text into the bounding area from practically any other application; or import text from a file, such as a Microsoft Word document.

To import text from a Microsoft Word document, choose File > Place and choose the Word document from the dialog box. In the dialog box that appears, choose whether to preserve formatting. (The option is off by default.)

In 1965 at Herbert Hoover Elementary School, Janice Jones was the reigning queen of the tetherball poles. She was the tallest girl in the entire fifth grade. She was beautiful and athletic with long brown hair and tan skin. She was also my best friend. As soon as the recess bell rang and the kids poured out of the doors onto the playground, Janice and I would rush towards the tetherball courts. The tetherball rules at our school went like this. The first two people to get to the court would play a game. (Janice and I

Fill the bounding area with text

Improving text justification

Wrapping a paragraph of justified text around an image can often result in undesirable spacing, with rivers of white space between the words. You can improve the justification. Illustrator has a feature called Every-line Composer that analyzes all of the lines in a paragraph (instead of just one), to make justified type more legible and easier to read. Turn on this feature by selecting your paragraph of text and choosing Every-line Composer from the Paragraph palette menu.

In 1965 at Herbert Hoover Elementary School, Janice Jones was the reigning queen of the tetherball poles. She was the tallest girl in the entire fifth grade. Janice was beautiful and athletic with long brown hair and tan skin. She was also my best friend. As soon as the recess bell rang and the kids poured out of the doors onto the playground, Janice and I would rush

Single-line Composer

In 1965 at Herbert Hoover Elementary School, Janice Jones was the reigning queen of the tetherball poles. She was the tallest girl in the entire fifth grade. Janice was beautiful and athletic with long brown hair and tan skin. She was also my best friend. As soon as the recess bell rang and the kids poured out of the doors onto the playground, Janice and I would rush towards the

Every-line Composer

Aligning margins optically

When you justify a body of type, you want the left and right margins to look perfectly straight. However, certain characters (punctuation, hyphens, quotation marks, and some letters of the alphabet) may cause an optical illusion and make the margins appear not very straight at all. To make the margins appear optically straight, select the text box with the selection or direct selection tool and choose Type > Optical Margin Alignment.

"In 1965 at Herbert Hoover Elementary School, Janice Jones was the reigning queen of the tetherball poles. She was the tallest girl in the entire fifth grade. Janice was beautiful, athletic and had long brown hair and tan skin. She was also my best friend. As soon as the recess bell rang and the kids poured out of the doors onto the playground, Janice and I would rush

Optical Margin Alignment off

"In 1965 at Herbert Hoover Elementary School, Janice Jones was the reigning queen of the tetherball poles. She was the tallest girl in the entire fifth grade. Janice was beautiful, athletic and had long brown hair and tan skin. She was also my best friend. As soon as the recess bell rang and the kids poured out of the doors onto the playground, Janice and I would rush towards the

Optical Margin Alignment on

3 Command/Ctrl-click outside of the text area. Then use the type tool to create the initial cap for your paragraph. It can be any combination of text and art (vector or raster).

4 Click the selection tool. Choose Type > Create Outlines to convert the type to outlines. This step is necessary because the text wrap feature will wrap around the bounding box of a type object. The font's bounding box is often much larger than the desired wrap.

5 Create a rectangle to act as a bounding box around the letterform. Choose Object > Arrange > Send To Back to move the rectangle behind the letterform. Paint the rectangle if desired. When you have completed the art, group together all elements of the initial cap.

6 Move your initial cap art and position it where you'd like, overlapping the paragraph text in the Area Text box.

7 If the initial cap isn't in front of the paragraph text, choose Object > Arrange > Bring to Front. For the text wrap to work, the initial cap must be above the paragraph text in the object stacking order, and the initial cap and paragraph text must be on the same layer.

Position the initial cap art above the text

8 With just the initial cap group selected, choose Object > Text Wrap > Make Text Wrap to display the Text Wrap Options dialog box. Turn on the Preview option so that you can see how the text will wrap as you adjust the Offset value. When you're satisfied with the value, click OK.

9 Use the type tool to remove the first letter in the paragraph to avoid repeating the initial cap. With the selection tool, continue to position the initial cap and the paragraph independently; the text wrap will update automatically.

Enter the Offset amount

n 1965 at Herbert Hoover Elementary School, Janice Jones was the reigning queen of the tetherball poles. She was the tallest girl in the entire fifth grade. Janice was beautiful and athletic with long brown hair and tan skin. She was also my best friend. As soon as the recess bell rang and the kids poured out of the doors onto the playground, Janice and I would rush towards the tetherball courts. The

Completed rectangular text wrap

Selecting groups

You can easily tell what you have selected by looking at the Appearance palette. Notice that if you click a group in the artwork with the selection tool, the Appearance palette shows that the Group item is selected. If you click a group in the artwork with the direct selection tool, the Appearance palette indicates that something else is selected (such as a path or type).

Group selected with the selection tool

Group selected with the direct selection tool

Illustrator calculates the text wrap around the bounding box of your initial cap. If you have a drop shadow or other effects applied to your art, the offset may be too far away from the text. When specifying an Offset amount for your text wrap, you can specify negative numbers to compensate.

I n 1965 at Herbert Hoover Elementary School, Janice Jones was the reigning queen of the tetherball poles. She was the tallest girl in the entire fifth grade. Janice was beautiful, athletic and had long brown hair and tan skin. She was also my best friend. As soon as the recess bell rang and the kids poured out of the doors

3-point offset

I n 1965 at Herbert Hoover Elementary School, Janice Jones was the reigning queen of the tetherball poles. She was the tallest girl in the entire fifth grade. Janice was beautiful, athletic and had long brown hair and tan skin. She was also my best friend. As soon as the recess bell rang and the kids poured out of the doors onto the

–1-point offset

Variation: Contoured text wrap

Some drop caps are simply enlarged characters with no surrounding art. You may want the text wrap to match the distinct outline of a character (called a glyph), rather than have text wrap around a bounding box.

1   Convert the drop cap to outlines by selecting the letterform with the selection tool. Then choose Type > Create Outlines.

2   Apply the text wrap by following steps 6 and 7 of the Rectangular Text Wrap technique.

I n 1965 at Herbert Hoover Elementary School, Janice Jones was the reigning queen of the tetherball poles. She was the tallest girl in the entire fifth grade. Janice was beautiful and athletic with long brown hair and tan skin. She was also my best friend. As soon as the recess bell rang and the kids poured out of the doors onto the playground, Janice and I would rush towards the tetherball courts. The tetherball rules at our school went like this. The first

Completed contoured text wrap

Text wrap around an entire word

Some designs call for wrapping text around the first word instead of just the first character of a paragraph. Here's a technique using the Appearance palette that will automatically adapt to any word you use. Similar to the Rectangular Text Wrap technique, this technique has the advantage of keeping the type editable. The disadvantage is that you have less control over the exact size and shape of the rectangle.

1   Using the type tool, enter the word around which you will
    wrap text. Style it with the desired font and size, and color
    it other than black (so that it will be easier to see as you
    work).

1965, Herbert Hoover Elementary School, Janice
Jones was the reigning queen of the tetherball poles.
She was the tallest girl in the entire fifth grade.
Janice was beautiful and athletic with long brown
hair and tan skin. She was also my best friend. As
soon as the recess bell rang and the kids poured out
of the doors onto the playground, Janice and I would
rush towards the tetherball courts. The tether-ball
rules at our school went like this. The first two
people to get to the court would play a game. (Janice
and I always tried to be first.) The player who
wrapped the tethered ball all the way around the

Create the first word

2   Use the selection tool to select the text. Choose Window >
    Appearance to open the Appearance palette. From the
    palette menu, choose Add New Fill.

Notice that your text is now colored black again. This is because
the new fill you just added is above it in the stacking order.

3   In the Appearance palette, drag the black Fill item to
    beneath the Characters item. You should now see the text in
    the color that you chose in step 1.

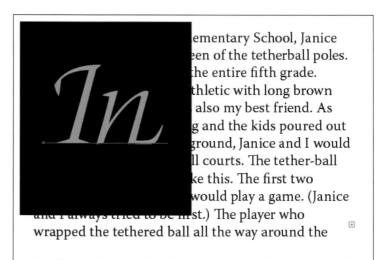

Add a new fill

Move the fill below the Characters item

4 Click the black Fill item listed in the Appearance palette to select it, and choose Effect > Convert to Shape > Rectangle. Turn on the Preview option. Then choose the Relative option and click OK.

The Relative option makes the rectangle that now appears behind your text grow or shrink as you edit the text.

ementary School, Janice
een of the tetherball poles.
the entire fifth grade.
thletic with long brown
also my best friend. As
g and the kids poured out
ground, Janice and I would
ll courts. The tether-ball
ke this. The first two
would play a game. (Janice
and I always tried to be first.) The player who
wrapped the tethered ball all the way around the

Apply the Convert to Shape effect

5 For a stylized appearance, select the fill and change its color; or apply other effects to it, such as Scribble.

Select the Fill item   *Change the color or add an effect*

6 Apply the text wrap by following steps 6 through 9 of the Rectangular Text Wrap technique.

1965 at Herbert Hoover Elementary School, Janice Jones was the reigning queen of the tetherball poles. She was the tallest girl in the entire fifth grade. Janice was beautiful and athletic with long brown hair and tan skin. She was also my best friend.

As soon as the recess bell rang and the kids poured

Completed wraparound word

Text as a container

In the Text Wrap Around an Entire Word technique, selecting the type with the selection tool makes the color preview in the toolbar display the color of the rectangle, even though the type appears in a different color on your screen. That's because in Illustrator a text object is a container—that means that the text object has two attributes: the type object itself and the characters within it. To see (and edit) a character's true colors, select the character with the type tool, not the selection tool; or double-click the Characters item in the Appearance palette.

Type selected with selection tool

Type selected with type tool

Text-heavy charts

Estimated Use of Water in the United States in 2000

[Data for 1995 and earlier from Solley and others (1998). The water-use data are in billion gallons per day (thousand million gallons per day) and are rounded to two significant figures for 1950-80, and to three significant figures for 1985-2000; percentage change is calculated from unrounded numbers. —, not available] All figures from the United State Geological Survey.

	YEAR											PERCENTAGE CHANGE
	1950[1]	1955[2]	1960[3]	1965[4]	1970[4]	1975[5]	1980[3]	1985[3]	1990[3]	1995[3]	2000[3]	1995-2000
Population, in millions	150.7	164.0	179.3	193.8	205.9	216.4	229.6	242.4	252.3	267.1	285.3	+7
Offstream use:												
Total withdrawals	180	240	270	310	370	420	440	399	408	402	408	+2
Public supply	14	17	21	24	27	29	34	36.5	38.5	40.2	43.3	+8
Rural domestic and livestock:												
Self-supplied domestic	2.1	2.1	2.0	2.3	2.6	2.8	3.4	3.32	3.39	3.39	3.72	+10
Livestock and aquaculture	1.5	1.5	1.6	1.7	1.9	2.1	2.2	54.47	4.50	5.49	(6)	—
Irrigation	89	110	110	120	130	140	150	137	137	134	137	+2
Industrial:												
Thermoelectric power use	40	72	100	130	170	200	210	187	195	190	195	+3
Other industrial use	37	39	38	46	47	45	45	30.5	29.9	29.1	(7)	—
Source of water:												
Ground:												
Fresh	34	47	50	60	68	82	83	73.2	79.4	76.4	83.4	+9
Saline	(8)	0.6	0.4	0.5	1.0	1.0	0.9	0.65	1.22	1.11	1.26	+14
Surface:												
Fresh	140	180	190	210	250	260	290	265	259	264	262	-1
Saline	10	18	31	43	53	69	71	59.6	68.2	59.7	61	+2

[1] 48 States and District of Columbia, and Hawaii
[2] 48 States and District of Columbia
[3] 50 States and District of Columbia, Puerto Rico, and U.S. Virgin Islands
[4] 50 States and District of Columbia, and Puerto Rico
[5] From 1985 to present this category includes water use for fish farms
[6] Data not available for all States; partial total was 5.46
[7] Commercial use not available; industrial and mining use totaled 23.2
[8] Data not available

Presenting a lot of text information in a chart or table can often enhance readability and get your point across in a clear and understandable way. Creating these text-heavy charts can also be time consuming—but they don't have to be. Using paragraph, character, and graphic styles together, you can use Illustrator to get consistent and impressive results. Most text charts begin their lives in Microsoft Excel. You can copy and paste data from Excel into Illustrator, but unlike Microsoft Word, you can't place an Excel file.

Text-heavy chart

1   Copy the data for your chart from Microsoft Excel. Then switch to Illustrator. Click once with the type tool to get an insertion point; or drag to create an area text box or click an object to define it as a text box. Then paste the data.

Note: If you paste without an insertion point, the data from Excel will be pasted as individual text blocks and will be difficult to work with.

Once you have imported your text, you can begin to format and style the text using paragraph styles.

Creating a chart using area type

If your text chart will consist of equal-length entries, an alternate way to create the chart is by entering text in an area text box. Then choose Area Type Options from the Type menu to split the text box into the desired number of rows and columns.

This approach treats all of the text as one paragraph. Text flows from one "cell" to the next. For example, list pertinent data in the first column, continue with the appropriate items in the second column, and so on. To force text into a new row or column, insert the appropriate number of carriage returns. (Do not use tabs in the text file to separate entries.)

Yet another alternative: Lay out the chart using the powerful table editor feature in InDesign.

STS-1   April 12, 1981   Lots of debris damage. 300 tiles replaced.
STS-7   June 18, 1983   First known left bipod ramp foam shedding event.
STS-27R December 2, 1988 Debris knocks off tile; structural damage and near burn through results.
STS-32R January 9, 1990   Second known left bipod ramp foam event.
STS-35   December 2, 1990 First time NASA calls foam debris "safety of flight issue," and "re-use or turnaround issue."
STS-42   January 22, 1992   First mission after which the next mission (STS-45) launched without debris In-Flight Anomaly closure/resolution.
STS-45   March 24, 1992   Damage to wing RCC Panel 10-right. Unexplained Anomaly, "most likely orbital debris."

Copy chart text from Excel and paste it into Illustrator

Taking advantage of OpenType features

More so in charts than other design projects, you may need to use fractions, ordinals, and other special characters. Use OpenType fonts and then set OpenType options in your paragraph and character styles to get better-looking type with less work on your part. For more information on using OpenType fonts, see the OpenType Design technique on page 226.

NASA chart

OpenType Features

Figure: Default Figure

Position: Default Position

☑ Standard Ligatures   ☑ Ordinals
☑ Contextual Alternates ☑ Fractions
☐ Discretionary Ligatures
☐ Swash
☐ Stylistic Alternates
☐ Titling Alternates

Select OpenType features in the Paragraph Style Options dialog box

2 Choose Window > Type > Paragraph Styles to display the Paragraph Styles palette.

3 Select your text with the type tool. Then Option/Alt-click on the New Style button in the Paragraph Styles palette. This creates a new style and opens the Paragraph Style Options dialog box in one step. Name the style. Position the dialog box so that you can see your selected text on-screen and make sure that the Preview button in the lower left corner of the dialog box is selected.

Paragraph Style Options

Style Name: NASA chart

General	General
Basic Character Formats	
Advanced Character Formats	Style Settings: [Normal Paragraph Style] +
Indents and Spacing	
Tabs	▼ Basic Character Formats
Composition	Font Family:Myriad
Hyphenation	Font Style:Roman
Justification	Size:9 pt
Character Color	Kerning:0 (zero)
OpenType Features	Tracking:0
	▼ Advanced Character Formats
	Horizontal Scale:100%

☑ Preview   (Reset Panel)   (Cancel)   (OK)

Create a new paragraph style

4 In the Paragraph Style Options dialog box, click the Basic Character Formats tab in the list on the left. Select the font you want to use and any other basic settings, such as size and leading, within each entry.

Paragraph Style Options

Style Name: NASA chart

General	Basic Character Formats
Basic Character Formats	
Advanced Character Formats	Font Family: Myriad Pro
Indents and Spacing	Font Style: Condensed
Tabs	
Composition	Size: 9 pt Leading: 13 pt
Hyphenation	Kerning: Auto Tracking: 0
Justification	
Character Color	Case: Normal Position: Normal
OpenType Features	☐ Standard Vertical Roman Alignment

☑ Preview   (Reset Panel)   (Cancel)   (OK)

Specify basic character formatting

5   Continuing in the same dialog box, click the Tabs tab in the list on the left. Set your tab stops by selecting the desired tab icon, clicking just above the ruler, and dragging the arrow to the desired tab stop. You can set left, center, right, and alignment tabs (which align to a specified character, such as a decimal). Watch the preview so that you can see where best to place the tabs. (To remove a tab, drag it out of the ruler.)

6   Click the Indents and Spacing tab to specify values between entries using the Space Before or Space After fields. If you plan to use a separator or a rule between entries, make sure that there's enough space for the text to breathe. Click OK to define the style and apply it to your text.

Specify the indents and spacing

Using tab leaders

To help the reader follow related items in columnar lists across the page, you can use a filler that runs from one tab to another. So-called tab leaders are often used in charts or long lists of names and numbers such as a table of contents.

To assign a tab leader, follow these steps:

1 Select the type and choose Window > Type > Tabs to open the tab ruler.

Chapter 10	238
Chapter 11	265
Chapter 12	299
Chapter 13	328
Index	359
Colophon	388

Original text

2 Select the tab above the ruler to which you want to add a leader. In the Leader field, enter a character. The example here shows a leader consisting of a period (.) and three spaces.

Highlight the tab and enter the leader characters

3 Press Return/Enter to apply the leader to the selected text.

Chapter 10	238
Chapter 11	265
Chapter 12	299
Chapter 13	328
Index	359
Colophon.	388

Text with tab leaders

STS-1	April 12, 1981	Lots of debris damage. 300 tiles replaced.
STS-7	June 18, 1983	First known left bipod ramp foam shedding event.
STS-27R	December 2, 1988	Debris knocks off tile; structural damage and near burn through results.
STS-32R	January 9, 1990	Second known left bipod ramp foam event.
STS-35	December 2, 1990	First time NASA calls foam debris "safety of flight issue," and "re-use or turnaround issue."
STS-42	January 22, 1992	First mission after which the next mission (STS-45) launched without debris In-Flight Anomaly closure/resolution.
STS-45	March 24, 1992	Damage to wing RCC Panel 10-right. Unexplained Anomaly, "most likely orbital debris."

Apply the paragraph style to the chart text

7 If the text fits all the width of all of the columns, skip to step 8. If any column has too much text to fit into the column width, at the end of the first line press Shift+Return/Enter to add a return without adding extra leading; then press Tab as needed to align the additional lines of text correctly.

In the following example, Shift+Return/Enter was applied to the third, fifth, sixth, and seventh entries. Then two tabs were entered to move the text to the third column. Notice that the second line of these entries uses the leading amount within entries that was specified in step 4; the spacing specified in step 6 for between entries is only added at the end of the entry.

STS-1	April 12, 1981	Lots of debris damage. 300 tiles replaced.
STS-7	June 18, 1983	First known left bipod ramp foam shedding event.
STS-27R	December 2, 1988	Debris knocks off tile; structural damage and near burn through results.
STS-32R	January 9, 1990	Second known left bipod ramp foam event.
STS-35	December 2, 1990	First time NASA calls foam debris "safety of flight issue," and "re-use or turnaround issue."
STS-42	January 22, 1992	First mission after which the next mission (STS-45) launched without debris In-Flight Anomaly closure/resolution.
STS-45	March 24, 1992	Damage to wing RCC Panel 10-right. Unexplained Anomaly, "most likely orbital debris."

Add custom returns to chart entries as needed

8 Deselect your text. To emphasize a column of your chart, use the Character Styles palette (Window > Type > Character Styles). Option/Alt-click the New Style button at the bottom of the Character Styles palette. Set the text options as desired, name the style, and then click OK to define the style.

9 Select the text you want emphasized and apply the character style you just created in step 8 by clicking the style in the Character Styles palette. Notice that the selected text changes, but the paragraph style is not affected.

Here the font was changed to a bold sans-serif face (Myriad Pro Black Condensed) and decreased in size.

Creating a variety of tab leaders

Tab leaders can contain more than one character. If a normal dot leader appears too tight, specify a dot and a space or two as your leader—to space out the dots for a cleaner look. Other special characters such as bullets, brackets, asterisks, and so on, can make interesting tab leaders. You can also use the Glyphs palette (Window > Type > Glyphs) to find interesting alternatives. When using characters that sit too high, select the tab character in the text and choose Subscript from the Character palette menu.

Here are some character combinations you can try:

Chapter 10	238
Chapter 11	265

(_) Underscore character

Chapter 10	238
Chapter 11	265

(*) Asterisk character with subscript applied

Chapter 10	238
Chapter 11	265

(°) Degree symbol character plus two spaces with subscript applied

Chapter 10 ~ ~ ~ ~ ~ ~	238
Chapter 11 ~ ~ ~ ~ ~ ~	265

(~) Tilde character with one space

Chapter 10››››››››››››››››	238
Chapter 11››››››››››››››››	265

(›) Right angle bracket character

Kerning optically

When you define a paragraph or character style, choose Optical Kerning for better looking type. By analyzing the individual glyph shapes, Illustrator automatically adjusts the kerning for each letter, to produce evenly spaced, eye-pleasing text.

Create a new character style

STS-1	April 12, 1981	Lots of debris damage. 300 tiles replaced.
STS-7	June 18, 1983	First known left bipod ramp foam shedding event.
STS-27R	December 2, 1988	Debris knocks off tile; structural damage and near burn through results.
STS-32R	January 9, 1990	Second known left bipod ramp foam event.
STS-35	December 2, 1990	First time NASA calls foam debris "safety of flight issue," and "re-use or turnaround issue."
STS-42	January 22, 1992	First mission after which the next mission (STS-45) launched without debris In-Flight Anomaly closure/resolution.
STS-45	March 24, 1992	Damage to wing RCC Panel 10-right. Unexplained Anomaly, "most likely orbital debris."

Apply a character style to a column

Divider rules

To complete your chart, you can add rules to divide entries. Here's how to create a Scotch rule.

1   Use the pen tool to draw a 2-point rule with a black stroke and no fill between the entries you want to divide (here, between the heading and entries).

2 Choose Window > Appearance to display the Appearance palette. From the palette menu, choose Add New Stroke to add a second stroke. Paint it white and set its width to 1 point.

Add a white stroke   *Set the path's blend mode to Darken*

3 To make the white gap between the rules transparent, click the Path item in the Appearance palette (to select the entire path, not just the white stroke). In the Transparency palette (Window > Transparency), set the blend mode to Darken.

4 Choose Window > Graphic Styles to open the Graphic Styles palette. Using the selection tool, drag the Scotch rule into the Graphic Styles palette to define it as a style. Double-click the new style and name it. You can now apply this style to other rules that you draw in your chart.

Mission	Date	Description
STS-1	April 12, 1981	Lots of debris damage. 300 tiles replaced.
STS-7	June 18, 1983	First known left bipod ramp foam shedding event.
STS-27R	December 2, 1988	Debris knocks off tile; structural damage and near burn through results.
STS-32R	January 9, 1990	Second known left bipod ramp foam event.
STS-35	December 2, 1990	First time NASA calls foam debris "safety of flight issue," and "re-use or turnaround issue."
STS-42	January 22, 1992	First mission after which the next mission (STS-45) launched without debris In-Flight Anomaly closure/resolution.

Completed chart with a Scotch rule

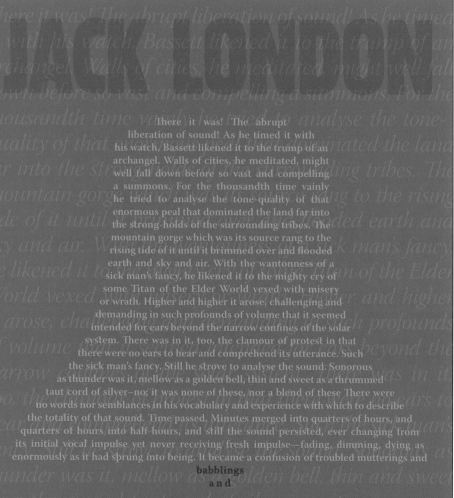

You can pour text into a shape using the area text tool. But did you know that you can flow text from one text-on-a-path to another? Not only that, you can also use curved paths to flow the threaded text along. In this technique you will create a shape guide first. Then you'll create the paths within that guide along which your text will flow. The paths can be curved or straight. You'll then flow the text along those paths and thread them together for easy editing. Never before has it been so easy to use text as an illustrative element.

Custom text shape and paths

1   Using the pen tool or the shape tools, create the shape that will define the outer borders of the text shape. Don't worry about its fill or stroke colors because you will make it into a guide in the next step.

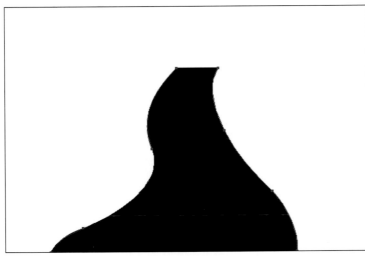

Create the shape that will define the text shape

2   With the shape still selected, choose View > Guides > Make Guides.

Using area text in a custom shape

Instead of tweaking each line's shape, here's how to flow your text into a shape.
1   Create a shape that will contain the text.

Create the shape for your text

2   Select the area text tool in the toolbox. Click the shape and enter the text.

Enter the text with the area text tool

3   Click in the text and choose Select > All. Use the Paragraph palette to adjust the alignment, and the Character palette to adjust the font, size, and leading settings until the text fits within the shape to your satisfaction.

Adjust the settings to fit the text within the shape

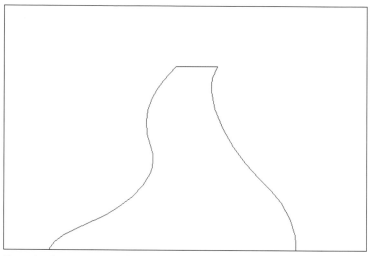

Turn the shape into a guide

3 Select the pen tool in the toolbox. Draw a line that has its beginning and ending point near the top of the shape guide.

This will be the baseline for the top line of text in your shape. The line can be straight or curved.

4 Click the pen tool in the toolbox to be able to start a new path. Draw a line that has its beginning and ending point near the bottom of the shape guide.

This will be the baseline for the bottom line of text in your shape. The line can be straight or curved.

5 Select both lines and choose Object > Blend > Make.

6 Choose Object > Blend > Blend Options and select Specified Steps for the Spacing option. Turn on the Preview option. Enter the number of lines of text you want minus two (the existing baselines for the top and bottom lines) and click OK.

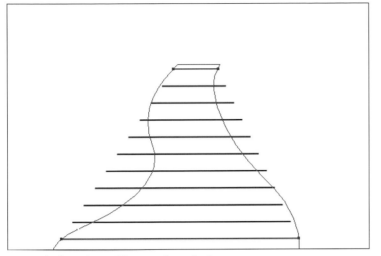

Create the lines that will become the paths for your text

7 Choose Object > Expand to expand the blend into separate lines.

These lines will be used as the paths for your lines of text.

Expand the blend

Using Smart Punctuation

Once you've created a lot of text on the page, it's a good idea to apply the Smart Punctuation command. This command gives you the option of replacing ligatures, curly quotation marks, spaces, dashes, and other typographic finesses. You can use it on the whole document or just on some selected text. To apply the command, choose Type > Smart Punctuation. Select the options you want and click OK. If you want a report on what was changed, select the Report Results option.

Apply the Smart Punctuation command

Editing text threads

If you have several text objects threaded together, here's how to remove one of the objects without losing the text flow or releasing the threading.

1 Select the object you want to remove from the thread with the selection tool.

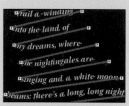

Select the object to be removed from the thread

2 Choose Type > Threaded Text; choose an option:
   - Release Section to remove just that path from the thread.
   - Remove Threading to release all sections from threading but keep the type in position.

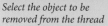

Release Section option

Remove Threading option

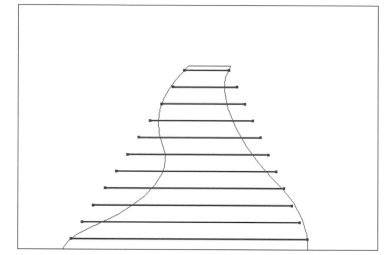

Ungroup the paths

8 Select the direct selection tool in the toolbox. Select the left endpoint of the second line from the top. Shift-drag it until it snaps to the left guide edge. (Hint: Start dragging the point and then press Shift to constrain the movement.)

9 Select the right endpoint of the second line from the top. Shift-drag it until it snaps to the right guide edge.

10 Repeat steps 8 and 9 for each line until all the lines fit perfectly inside the shape guide. You are now ready to start adding the text.

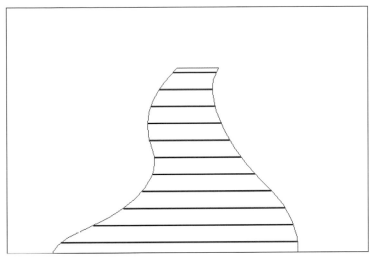

Adjust the lines to fit inside of the shape guide

Threaded text

1   Using the type tool, create a text area and enter the text that
    you will flow into a shape. Using the Character palette, give
    the type the size, font that you want. Apply a fill color. With
    the type tool, click anywhere in the type block and choose
    Select > All.

There's a long, long trail a-
winding into the land of my
dreams, where the nightingales
are singing and a white moon
beams: there's a long, long night
of waiting until my dreams all
come true; till the day when I'll
be going down that long long trail
with you. —Stoddard King, The
Long, Long Trail

Select all of the type

2   Choose Edit > Copy to copy the text.

3   Select the selection tool in the toolbox; then select the type tool. (You will need that selection tool later, and Illustrator remembers the last selection tool you used.) Position the type tool on the left side of the first line inside the shape guide. Notice that the type pointer changes to the type on a path pointer when you move it on top of the line. Click the left side of the line and choose Edit > Paste to add the text to that path.

All the text won't fit on that first line. Notice that a red plus sign appears to indicate that there is overflow text. You will continue to thread the text to the other lines in the next steps.

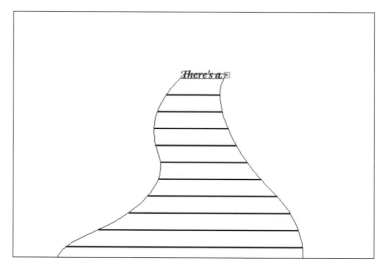

Add the text to the first line

4   With the type tool still active, press Command/Ctrl to switch temporarily to the selection tool. Click once on the red plus sign at the end of the first line. Release Command/Ctrl and notice that the pointer has changed to the loaded text icon.

5 Position the loaded text icon on the beginning of the second line within the shape guide. Click once to thread the text from the first line to that second line.

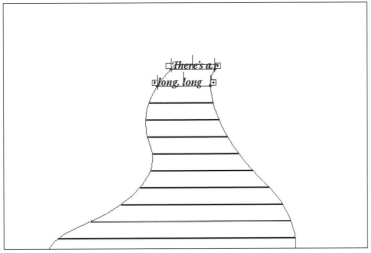

Thread the text to the second line

6 Notice that the tool has changed to the selection tool in the toolbox. Click the red plus sign at the end of the second line. Position the loaded text cursor over the third line and click to thread the text to that line. Repeat this step for each successive line in the shape guide. Don't worry if there is too much text for the lines or if the text didn't fill all the lines. Thread all the lines anyway. You will adjust the type size in subsequent steps.

Adding curves to a straight text path

You may have applied text to a straight path, but you can still give that path some curves. Here's how to do it:

1 Using the direct selection tool, select the path.

Direct-select the path

2 Select the convert anchor point tool in the toolbox (beneath the pen tool). Click one of the endpoints of the path and drag to change its curve.

Convert the endpoint to a curve anchor point

3 Repeat step 2 for the other endpoint on the path. If desired, use the add anchor point tool to add points to the path.

Convert the other endpoint to a curve anchor point

Copyfitting with decimals

When you are trying to fine-tune the fit of text into a shape, you may need to use a type size that includes decimals. If 10-point type is too small but 11-point type is too big, try using 10.5-point type or even 10.43-point type. Keep changing the fraction until you have a perfect fit. You can enter more than 2 places in the decimal, but Illustrator will round to the nearest hundredth of a point. For example, if you enter 10.6823 points, Illustrator will round it to 10.68 points.

Thread the text to the subsequent lines

7   Select the type tool in the toolbox, click anywhere in the type block, and choose Select > All. Using the Character palette, change the type size until it fits into the shape well.

The example below uses 6.6-point Warnock Semibold Italic. Depending on how closely you want the type to adhere to the shape guide, you may want to choose justified alignment instead of flush left alignment in the Paragraph palette.

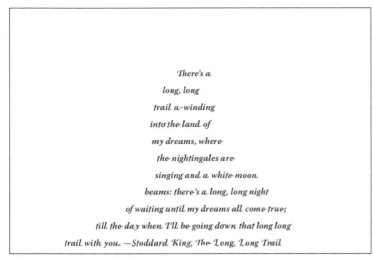

There's a
long, long
trail a-winding
into the land of
my dreams, where
the nightingales are
singing and a white moon
beams: there's a long, long night
of waiting until my dreams all come true;
till the day when I'll be going down that long long
trail with you. —Stoddard King, The Long, Long Trail

Adjust the type size to fit the shape

8 Add the other graphics to complete the image. If desired, you can use the direct selection tool to move and edit the paths. In the example below, the paths were changed from straight to curved lines to give the impression of waves. For more information on how to change a straight path to a curved path, see "Adding curves to a straight text path" on page 223.

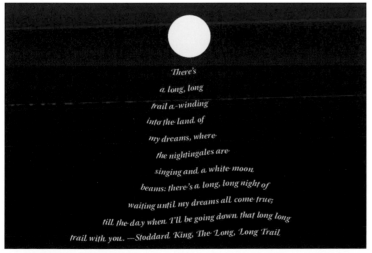

Completed text illustration

32 | OpenType design

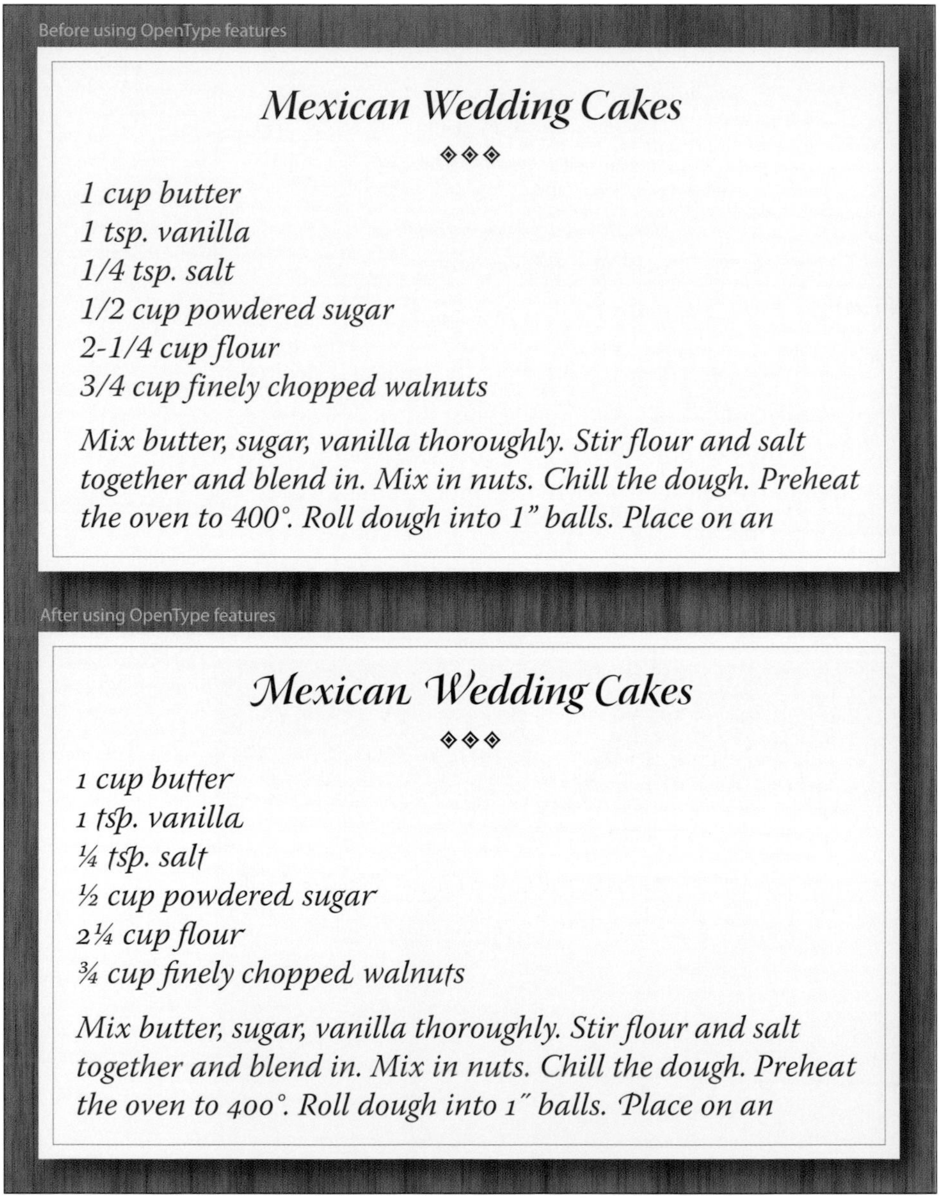

Mexican Wedding Cakes

❖ ❖ ❖

1 cup butter
1 tsp. vanilla
1/4 tsp. salt
1/2 cup powdered sugar
2-1/4 cup flour
3/4 cup finely chopped walnuts

Mix butter, sugar, vanilla thoroughly. Stir flour and salt together and blend in. Mix in nuts. Chill the dough. Preheat the oven to 400°. Roll dough into 1" balls. Place on an

Mexican Wedding Cakes

❖ ❖ ❖

1 cup butter
1 tsp. vanilla
¼ tsp. salt
½ cup powdered sugar
2¼ cup flour
¾ cup finely chopped walnuts

Mix butter, sugar, vanilla thoroughly. Stir flour and salt together and blend in. Mix in nuts. Chill the dough. Preheat the oven to 400°. Roll dough into 1″ balls. Place on an

The true art of typography has blossomed with the introduction of OpenType fonts. These fonts let you set distinctive type with easy, context-sensitive access to the individual characters (called glyphs) designed into a font. Able to contain up to 65,000 glyphs (PostScript Type 1 fonts max out at 256), OpenType fonts preserve the true intentions of the type designer with ligatures, true small caps, swash characters, stylistic alternates, fractions, and ordinals—all in a single cross-platform font file. Because a character can be represented by more than one glyph, you can substitute one version of a letterform for another.

This technique shows how to use OpenType fonts and Illustrator to add a professional touch to your type. You first specify an OpenType font and then apply any desired OpenType features. To fine-tune your type design, you can also browse through and substitute individual glyphs. And to save time, you can apply advanced OpenType options—such as swash alternates, discretionary ligatures, fractions, and ordinals—using paragraph or character styles.

OpenType features

1   Use the selection tool to select the text you want to format with OpenType fonts; if needed, use the type tool to create or import some text. With the text selected, use the Character palette (Window > Type > Character) to specify the Open Type font you want to use.

The following example uses Warnock Pro Italic and Semibold Italic Display, available separately from Adobe.

What does "Pro" mean?

OpenType fonts come in two varieties, standard and professional, and a font's name indicates which it is. Professional fonts follow their name with "Pro" (for example, Warnock Pro), and Standard fonts end with "Std" (for example, Frutiger Std). The word "Pro" indicates an OpenType font that can contain extended character sets and advanced layout features.

Identifying fonts easily

There's a good chance you have many fonts installed on your machine, including TrueType (TT), PostScript Type 1(A), Multiple Master (MM), and OpenType (O). You can easily tell the kind of font by the icon in the WYSIWYG Font menu (Type > Font).

> *a* Caslon Open Face
> ✓ *O* Adobe Caslon Pro
> T̂ Century Gothic
> *O* Century Old Style Std
> T̂ Chalkboard
> MM <Chaparral MM Expert>

Font icons in the Type list

Mexican Wedding Cakes

1 cup butter
1 tsp. vanilla
1/4 tsp. salt
1/2 cup powdered sugar
2-1/4 cup flour
3/4 cup finely chopped walnuts

Mix butter, sugar, vanilla thoroughly. Stir flour and salt together and blend in. Mix in nuts. Chill the dough. Preheat the oven to 400°. Roll dough into 1"

Spec type with OpenType fonts

2   Select a range of text that is formatted with an OpenType font.

3   Display the OpenType palette (Window > Type > OpenType). Choose the desired figure option (here, Proportional Oldstyle) from the Figure pop-up menu.

In the following example, the numbers in the recipe changed automatically on applying the Proportional Oldstyle figure option.

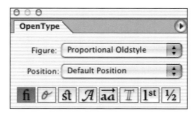

Choose a different Figure option

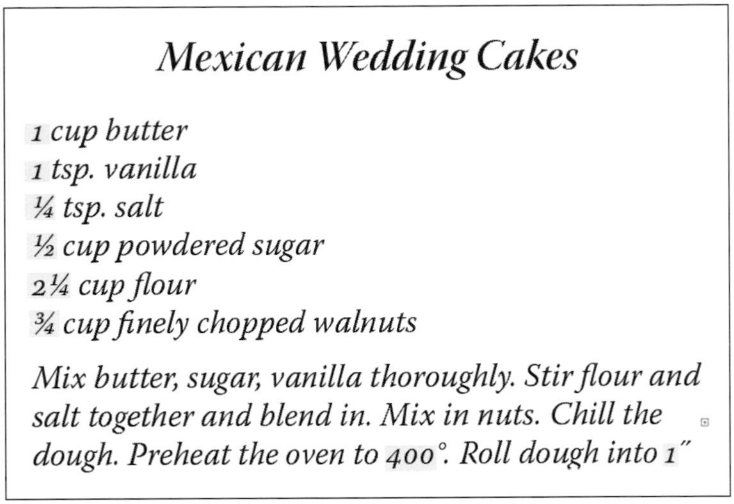
Mexican Wedding Cakes
1 cup butter
1 tsp. vanilla
¼ tsp. salt
½ cup powdered sugar
2¼ cup flour
¾ cup finely chopped walnuts
Mix butter, sugar, vanilla thoroughly. Stir flour and
salt together and blend in. Mix in nuts. Chill the
dough. Preheat the oven to 400°. Roll dough into 1″

Proportional Oldstyle figure option applied

4 With the text selection still active, click any of the icons along the bottom of the OpenType palette to apply specific glyph features. A highlighted icon means that feature is turned on for the selected text. A dimmed icon indicates that the selected OpenType font does not contain those special characters.

When designing a headline, logo, or paragraph of text, simply clicking the different icons can quickly give you an idea of what other glyphs are available for the selected text.

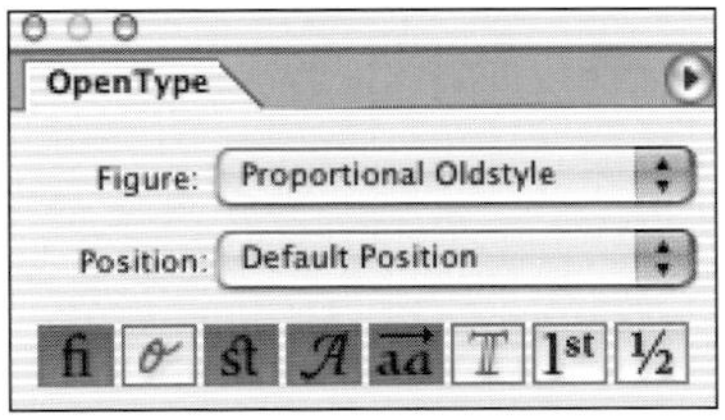
OpenType
Figure:
Proportional Oldstyle
Position:
Default Position

Turn on some of the special glyph features

Mexican Wedding Cakes

1 cup butter
1 tsp. vanilla
¼ tsp. salt
½ cup powdered sugar
2¼ cup flour
¾ cup finely chopped walnuts

Mix butter, sugar, vanilla thoroughly. Stir flour and salt together and blend in. Mix in nuts. Chill the dough. Preheat the oven to 400°. Roll dough into 1″

Discretionary ligatures, swash, and stylistic alternates features applied

Extended characters

It's convenient to apply OpenType features to entire text blocks, but you can also replace individual characters (called glyphs) to fine-tune your design. The Glyphs palette lets you browse through an entire font to find and apply alternate glyphs.

1   Use the type tool to select a character that you want to replace. To add a new character, use the type tool to click an insertion point.

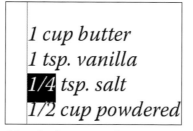

Select the character or characters you wish to replace

2   Choose Window > Type > Glyphs to display the Glyphs palette. The selected font's name appears in the pop-up menu at the bottom of the palette. Scroll through the glyphs until you find the one you want (an arrow indicates

alternate glyphs are available), and double-click it. The character will replace the selected glyph or appear at your insertion point.

Double-click the replacement glyph

3   Repeat steps 1 and 2 for each character that needs replacing. The following example shows all the fractions replaced and the quotation mark after the "1" changed to an inch mark.

Mexican Wedding Cakes

1 cup butter
1 tsp. vanilla
¼ tsp. salt
½ cup powdered sugar
2¼ cup flour
¾ cup finely chopped walnuts

Mix butter, sugar, vanilla thoroughly. Stir flour and salt together and blend in. Mix in nuts. Chill the dough. Preheat the oven to 400°. Roll dough into 1″

Fractions and inch mark replaced

Adjusting individual glyphs

If you applied a special glyph feature to an entire block of text, chances are that it won't look good in certain situations. If a glyph seems inappropriate, don't turn off the feature. Instead, simply select the undesired glyph and click the feature icon in the OpenType palette to toggle it off for that selection.

Glyph features applied to all text

Glyph features turned off for "butter," "salt," and "powdered"

OpenType style

Once you have fine-tuned your type design, you can save your work as a paragraph style to save time and ensure consistent formatting. Paragraph styles affect entire paragraphs. To apply a style just to selected text, rather than an entire paragraph, you can create a character style.

1 Choose Window > Type > Paragraph Styles to display the Paragraph Styles palette.

2 Select the text that you completed formatting with your OpenType Pro font.

3 To save the formatting as a paragraph style, Option/Alt-click the New Styles button at the bottom of the Paragraph Styles palette. In the Paragraph Style Options dialog box, name the style and click OK.

Create a new paragraph style

4 To apply the paragraph style, select the text using the type or selection tool; then click the style name in the Paragraph Styles palette.

5 To edit the style, double-click the style name in the Paragraph Styles palette. On the left side of the dialog box, click the OpenType Features tab. In the dialog box that appears, turn on the Preview option. Select or deselect the desired features, and click OK. Any options that you specify here will be applied to the style once you click OK.

Add OpenType features to the style

Creating a character style follows the same steps as creating a paragraph style, but uses the Character Styles palette. Follow steps 1 through 4, but select the characters desired for the style (rather than a paragraph) and then use the Character Styles palette (Window > Type > Character Styles) to create the style.

Mix butter, sugar, vanilla thoroughly. Stir flour and salt together and blend in. Mix in nuts. Chill the dough. Preheat the oven to 400°. Roll dough into 1″ balls. Place on an ungreased baking sheet. Bake for 10-12 minutes or until set but not brown. While still warm, roll in powdered sugar. Cool. Roll in sugar again. Yield: 4 dozen cookies.

Paragraph style using OpenType features

Section 5 | 3D effects

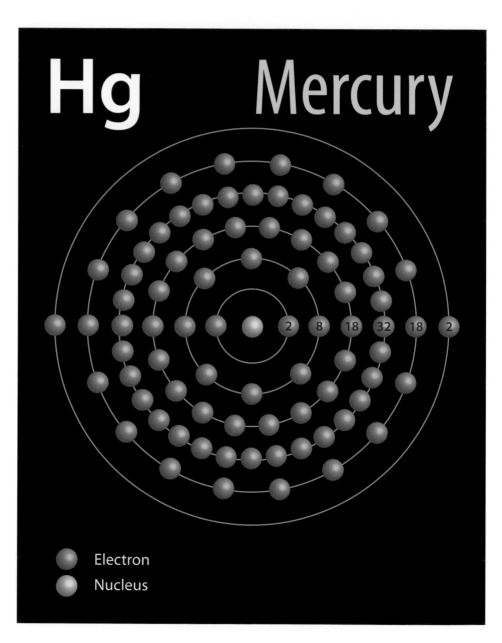

Sometimes you just need a quick 3D shape without custom bevels or several lights and mapped artwork. This technique shows you how to make four very basic shapes using the 3D effect: a cube, a cone, a sphere, and a cylinder. You'll start with a flat, painted shape and then apply the 3D effect to it: just enter a couple of settings and you've got an instant 3D object. Following are instructions for a cube, sphere, cone, and cylinder. You can customize them by changing the height and width, paint color, and lighting.

Cube

1   Select the rectangle tool in the toolbox. Click the artboard once to display the Rectangle dialog box. Enter the same amount for the width and height. Note this value for use in step 3. Click OK.

To make a cube, you extrude the square by the same amount as its width and height.

Create a square

2   With the square still selected, display the Color palette and give the square a color fill with a stroke of None.

When you use the 3D extrusion feature, stroked objects have the color of the stroke on the extruded side. The color of the fill only shows up on the front face of the cube. To make this cube the same color on all sides, you paint it with a stroke of None. For more information, see "Extruding with or without a stroke" on page 178.

Shortcut: Duplicate the width or height amount

When creating a square, rounded square, or circle, you need to enter only one amount. Select the rectangle, ellipse, or rounded rectangle tool in the toolbox. Click the artboard once. In the dialog box that appears, enter the number for the width. To duplicate that number for the height, simply click the word "Height" to enter the width amount automatically into the Height text box. This also works if you enter the height first and then click the word "Width."

Extruding a compound shape

Do you want to create a 3D shape that has a hole in the middle? Here's how to do it:

1 Create the outside shape with a shape tool or the pen tool.
2 Create the inside shape. Select both shapes.

Create the outer and inner shapes and select them

3 Choose Object > Compound Path > Make.

Create a compound path

4 With the compound path still selected, choose Effect > 3D > Extrude & Bevel.
5 Turn on the Preview option and enter an Extrude Depth amount. When you are satisfied with the effect, click OK.

Extruded compound shape

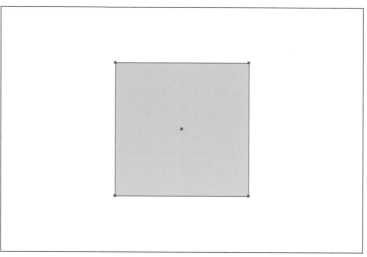

Paint the square with a color fill and a stroke of None

3 Choose Effect > 3D > Extrude & Bevel. Turn on the Preview option. Enter the amount you noted in step 1 as the extrude depth. If desired, adjust the lighting by clicking More Options and use the Surface options. Click OK to complete the cube. Deselect.

When you create a new object, Illustrator by default applies only the current paint attributes to the object—without any effects—to optimize performance. If you want to apply the current effects to new objects you create, deselect the New Art Has Basic Appearance option in the Appearance palette menu.

Extrude & Bevel

Extrude Depth: 100 pt ▶ Cap:

Bevel: None ▼

Height: 4 pt ▶

Surface: Plastic Shading ▲▼

Light Intensity: 100% ▶
Ambient Light: 50% ▶
Highlight Intensity: 60% ▶
Highlight Size: 90% ▶
Blend Steps: 50 ▶

Shading Color: Black ▲▼

☐ Preserve Spot Colors   ☐ Draw Hidden Faces

Apply the 3D Extrude & Bevel effect

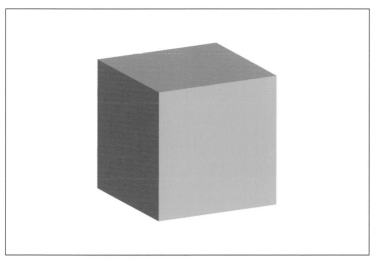

Completed cube

Cone

A cone is made by creating a triangle first and then revolving it with the 3D Revolve effect.

1   Select the pen tool in the toolbox. Click the artboard to create the top point of the cone (A). Then Shift-click at the point where the center of the cone base will be (B). Shift-click again to create the point where the outside edge of the base will be (C). Then close the path by clicking again on the original point (A).

You have just created a triangle that will be revolved to make a cone. The triangle is one-half the width that the cone will be.

2   With the triangle still selected, display the Color palette and give the triangle a color fill with a stroke of None.

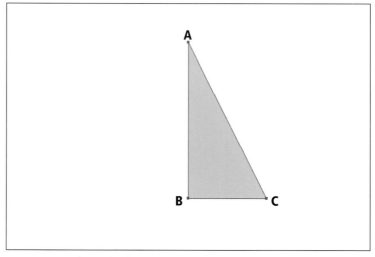

Create a triangle one-half the width of the cone

3   Choose Effect > 3D > Revolve. Turn on the Preview option. For a smoother appearance, increase the blend steps. In the following examples, 121 blend steps were used. Click OK. Deselect.

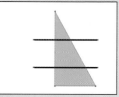

Apply the 3D Revolve effect

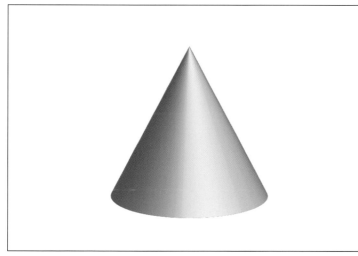

Completed cone

Creating striped cones

To add stripes or colored bands to a cone, create the stripes before you revolve.

1 Follow step 1 of the Cone technique to create a triangle.
2 Create some lines to divide the shape. You should have one less line than the number of stripes you want. Select the lines and the triangle.

Draw lines to divide the shape

3 Display the Pathfinder palette and click the Divide button.
4 Use the direct selection tool to select each stripe and change its color.

Select the triangle and lines

5 Follow step 3 of the Cone technique.

Completed striped cone

Cutaway spheres

If you want to see the core of a multilayered sphere, you need to create the different layers, group them, and then revolve. Here's how to do it:

1 Follow step 1 of the Sphere technique to create a circle.

2 Position the ellipse tool over the center point of the circle and Option/Alt-drag a new circle that is smaller.

3 Follow steps 3 and 4 of the Sphere technique to create and paint each half-circle.

4 Select the half-circles and group them.

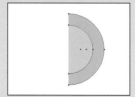

Select the half-circles group

5 Continue with step 5 of the Sphere technique to create the 3D sphere. Use a rotate angle of less than 360°. The example below uses an angle of 232°. Adjust the lighting and click OK.

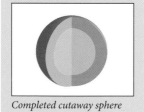

Completed cutaway sphere

Sphere

A sphere is made by creating a half circle first and then revolving it with the 3D Revolve effect.

1 Select the ellipse tool in the toolbox. Click the artboard to open the Ellipse dialog box. Enter equal amounts for the width and height of your sphere and click OK.

Create a circle

2 With the circle still selected, display the Color palette and give the circle a color fill with a stroke of None. Deselect.

3 Choose the direct selection tool in the toolbox. Select only the left point of the circle and press Delete/Backspace to remove it.

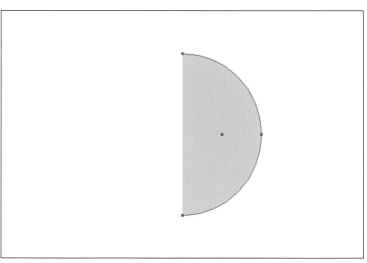

Delete the left point from the circle

4 With the direct selection tool, select the top and bottom points. Choose Object > Path > Join to close the path.

5   With the half circle still selected, choose Effect > 3D >
Revolve. Turn on the Preview option. For a smoother
appearance, increase the blend steps. In the following
example, 126 blend steps were used. Click OK when you are
satisfied with the preview. Deselect.

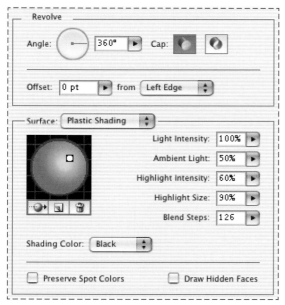

Apply the 3D Revolve effect

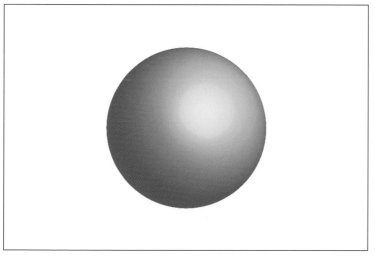

Completed sphere

Cylinder

A cylinder is made by creating a tall rectangle first and then revolving it with the 3D Revolve effect.

1   Select the rectangle tool in the toolbox. Click the artboard once to display the Rectangle dialog box. Enter the amount for the width and height, with the Width amount half the thickness of the desired cylinder. Click OK.

2   With the rectangle still selected, display the Color palette and give the rectangle a color fill with a stroke of None.

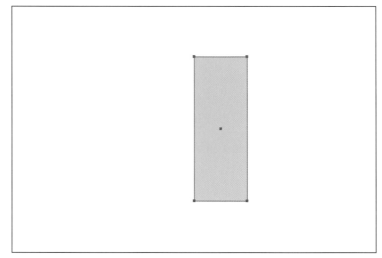

Create a rectangle one-half the width of the cylinder

3   Choose Effect > 3D > Revolve. Turn on the Preview option. For a smoother appearance, increase the blend steps. In the following examples, 121 blend steps were used. When you are satisfied with the preview, click OK.

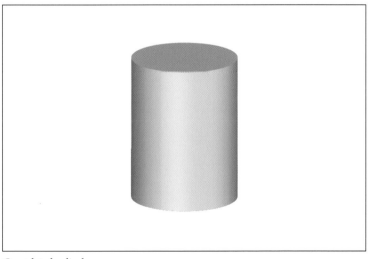

Apply the 3D Revolve effect

Completed cylinder

Time

It's all relative

6
5
4
3
2
1
0

Actual Minutes
Football minute
Design minute
Internet minute
Toothbrushing minute

Thank you for your time!

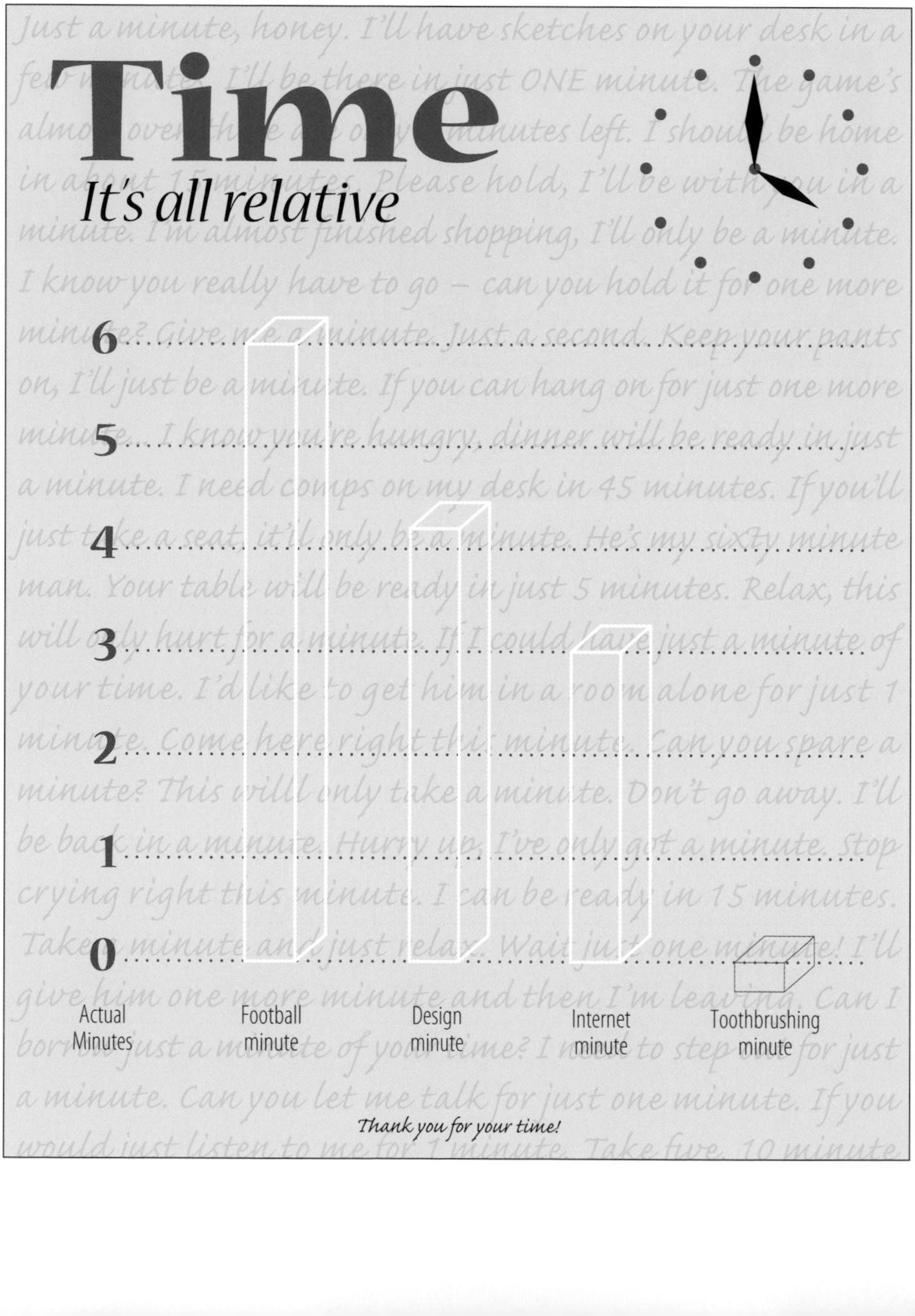

The graph tool in Adobe Illustrator creates flat, basic, functional graphs. The tool also is useful for calculating the correct ratio or size of the graphic elements. In this technique, create a basic bar chart and then design your own three-dimensional bar marker. The third dimension adds a little more visual interest, but be careful not to create a design that's too elaborate. The purpose of a bar chart is to represent information that can be easily compared. Simple bar designs work best!

Basic bar graph

1   Select the column graph tool in the toolbox. With the tool, drag an area the size that you want your graph to be. When you release the mouse button, the Graph Data window will appear along with a basic graph.

2   Enter the data for your graph. You can either enter the data manually or import it from another program. (For more information on how to import data, see Illustrator Help.) Use the far left column for the labels that appear at the bottom of each column on the graph. Enclose each label with quotation marks. (You can enter legends by using the top row and enclosing each legend in quotation marks.) Enter the data in the columns to the right of the labels column. Press Return/Enter or click Apply (the checkmark) in the Graph Data window.

Enter the labels and data in the Graph Data window

Using premade graph designs

You can choose a 3D sliding bar design from the premade designs that come with Illustrator CS. Here's how.

1   Choose File > Open and navigate to the Adobe Illustrator CS folder. Then choose Sample Files > Graph Designs > Column & Marker Designs1.ai or Column & Marker Designs2.ai.

2   Keep the file open as you work on your graph.

3   Choose Object > Graph > Coiumn and choose a design from the column design list.

Here are some of the choices.

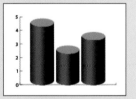

Cylinder column+

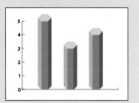

Hexagon+

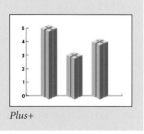

Plus+

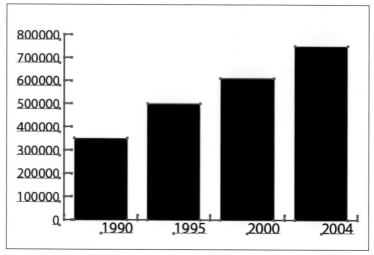

Default bar chart result

3   Close the Graph Data window to complete the data entry.

4   Select the group selection tool in the toolbox. Click one of the number labels to select it and then click again to select the entire group. Change the typeface, size, or alignment.

The following example shows the typeface changed, the lower labels centered, and commas and a dollar sign added to the side labels with the type tool.

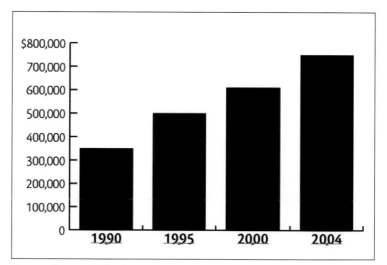

Format the type in the chart

Sliding 3D bar design

1   Use the Basic Bar Graph technique to create a bar chart. Using the View menu, turn on both the Snap to Point and Smart Guides options.

2   Use the direct selection tool to select the smallest column in the graph. Choose Edit > Copy and deselect the shape.

You choose the smallest column to ensure that the top and side designs don't overlap when you make the sliding line in step 10.

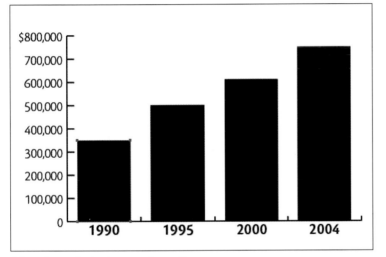

Select the smallest column and copy it

3   In the Layers palette, Option/Alt-click the New Layer button at the bottom of the palette to create a new layer, and name it Graph Design. Hide the layer containing the graph. Select the Graph Design layer and paste the rectangle onto it.

4   Paint the rectangle with a stroke and fill of None. Choose Edit > Copy to copy the rectangle.

This will become the bounding box for your bar design.

5   Choose Edit > Paste in Front to paste a copy of the bounding box directly on top of itself. Paint the rectangle

with the color you want for the face of the three-dimensional bars.

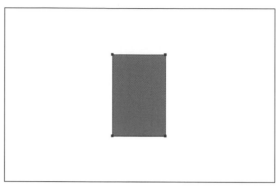

Paint the face of the three-dimensional column

6 With the rectangle still selected, select the scale tool and Option/Alt-click the upper left corner point of the rectangle. Choose Non-Uniform scale and enter a Horizontal value of 100% and a Vertical value of –20%. Click Copy. Paint the top with a different color. To paint with a tint of the original color, see the "Shortcut: Lighten or darken a CMYK color" on page 45.

This shape will become the top of the three-dimensional bar.

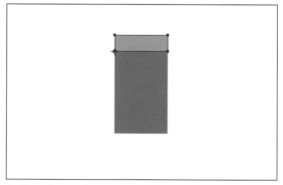

Scale and copy; then paint the new shape

7 Select the shear tool and click once on the same upper left point as you clicked in step 6. This sets the point of origin.

Then click the top right point of the top rectangle, hold down Shift, and drag along the 0° Smart Guide. Release the mouse button and then Shift when you are satisfied with the shear angle.

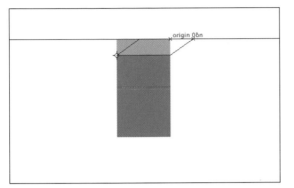

Shear the top shape

8   Choose the selection tool. Click one of the left corner points of the sheared top rectangle and drag to the right. Hold down Shift and Option/Alt to constrain it along the 0° Smart Guide and make a copy. When you reach the corresponding right corner point, release the mouse button and then Shift and Option/Alt.

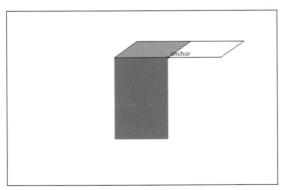

Duplicate the top shape

9   Use the direct selection tool to select the two rightmost anchor points of the copy you just made. Drag the front right point down until it snaps to the lower right corner

Using sliding column designs

Sliding column designs do not always fit the size of the graph. If you choose a sliding graph design that doesn't fit, you must adjust the column width. In the center illustration, notice how the right pencil looks turned inside out. Also, the sliding boundary guides are all higher than the tops of the columns. To fix these problems, do this:

1 Choose Object > Graph > Type.

2 Choose Graph Options from the pop-up menu.

3 In the Options section, decrease the Column Width percentage. Click OK.

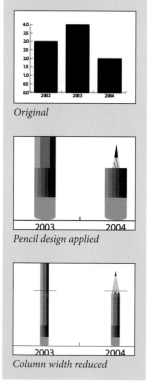

Original

Pencil design applied

Column width reduced

point of the bar. Paint the side of the column with a different color.

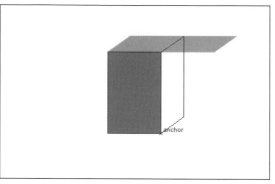

Pull the right edge down to the front face corner

10 Use the pen or line segment tool to draw a horizontal line that intersects the column design. Position the line between the top and bottom corner points. Select the line and the bar design and choose Object > Group.

This line will be the sliding boundary—a line below which the design will be vertically scaled in a graph. The area above the line won't change.

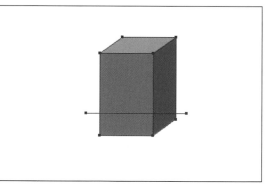

Create a horizontal line and group it with the column art

11 With the direct selection tool, select only the horizontal sliding line. Choose View > Guides > Make Guides.

The guide is grouped with the bar design. Even if the Lock
Guides option is turned on, the guide will still be selected when
the group is selected.

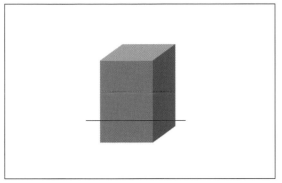

Make the horizontal line into a guide

12 Select the group and choose Object > Graph > Design.
Click the New Design button. Then click the Rename
button, and name the design 3D Bar. Click OK.

Save the column artwork as a graph design

New graph design

1 In the Layers palette, hide the Graph Design layer. Show the
layer containing the bar graph. Select the graph, and choose
Object > Graph > Column. Select the 3D Bar design, and
choose Sliding as the Column Type. Click OK.

Scaling graph columns

You can adjust the width of the graph column design if it is too wide or overlaps the other columns. Follow these steps.

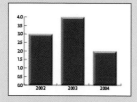

1 Choose Object > Graph > Type.
2 Choose Graph Options from the pop-up menu.
3 In the Options section, enter a different percentage for the Column Width. Click OK.

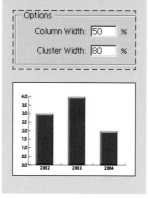

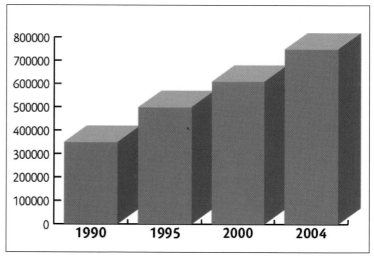

Change the column design to the 3D Bar design

2 Choose View > Guides > Hide Guides to evaluate the results.

The following example shows some problems with the graph: The bars are in front of the value axis (the *x* axis for bar graphs) line, and the commas and dollar sign disappeared during the column change. You will correct these problems in the last step.

Evaluate the results

3 If you are satisfied with the look of the bars, skip to step 6. If you want to change the color or size of the bars, show the Graph Design layer in the Layers palette.

4 Edit the bars' color or size, as desired. Then save the graph design artwork, following step 12 of the Sliding 3D Bar Design technique. Name the new design 3D Bar2.

5 Repeat steps 1 through 4 of this technique until you are satisfied with the graph design.

6 Adjust the position of the axis lines or bars, if needed, using the direct selection tool to select the shapes or lines and reposition them. You can also use the type tool to change the type style and copy. Add a title and save the file.

Finalize the column design before making these changes, because they will be lost if you edit the column design or change the data.

The following example was changed in these ways:

- The horizontal tick marks were lengthened and changed to dotted lines.

- The vertical tick marks were painted with no stroke.

- Each column was selected and scaled horizontally from its right bottom corner.

- The *x* and *y* axes were painted with no stroke.

- Type was edited and the typeface was changed.

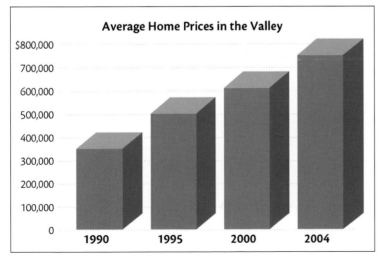

Completed bar chart

Hiding graph components

If you want to be able to keep editing a graph with the graph tools, hide—rather than delete—parts of the graph that you don't want or may want to edit later.

You can delete parts of a graph only after first ungrouping and then expanding the graph's contents. Once you ungroup a graph, you can no longer change its data, column designs, or legends. But if you hide graph components, you can edit them later. To hide parts of a graph, do this:

1 Choose the direct selection tool in the toolbox.
2 Select the object or objects in the graph that you want to hide.
3 In the Color palette, paint the objects with no stroke and no fill.

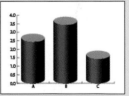

Default bar graph design

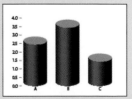

Axes and lower tick marks filled and stroked with None

35 | 3D pie charts

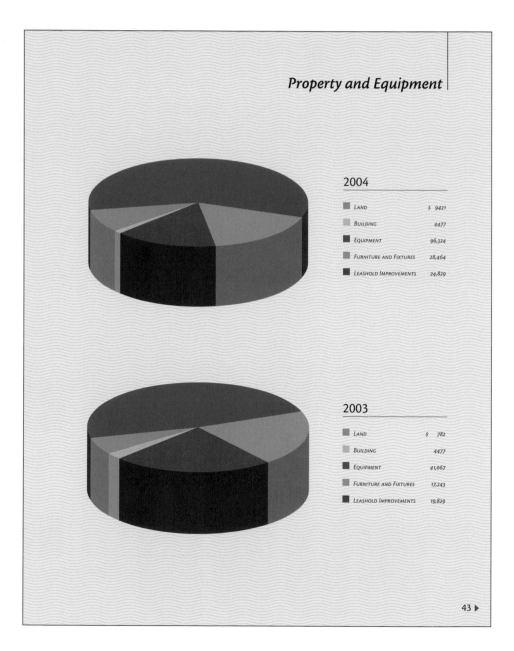

Property and Equipment

2004

▨	LAND	$ 9421
▨	BUILDING	4477
▪	EQUIPMENT	96,324
▨	FURNITURE AND FIXTURES	28,464
▪	LEASHOLD IMPROVEMENTS	24,829

2003

▨	LAND	$ 782
▨	BUILDING	4477
▪	EQUIPMENT	41,067
▨	FURNITURE AND FIXTURES	17,243
▪	LEASHOLD IMPROVEMENTS	19,829

Numerical data always is more exciting and relevant when presented in visual form. Pie charts can wake up a presentation and clearly indicate the point that you want to make. Adding a 3D aspect to pie charts can make them seemingly jump off the page. Using Illustrator's graphing capabilities coupled with its powerful 3D effects, you can quickly and easily add attention-getting pie charts to your design repertoire. For other ways to create graphs, see "3D bar charts" on page 246 and "Text-heavy charts" on page 208.

Pie chart

1   Select the pie graph tool. You can find it by positioning the mouse on the column graph tool and dragging to the right. The pie graph tool is the second to the last in the tool group.

Select the pie graph tool

2   With the pie graph tool selected, click once anywhere on-screen to create a graph and display the Graph dialog box where you can enter the dimensions for the chart. Because you will add 3D later, start with a circle for the graph by entering equal amounts for the width and height.

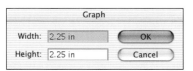

Enter the same amount for width and height

3   In the Graph Data window, enter the graph data using any of these methods: Type in the values in Illustrator; copy and paste an entire range of values from a Microsoft Excel file; or click the Import button in the Graph Data window

(the leftmost button at the top of the window) to choose a tab-delimited text file from an application such as Excel. You can import a tab-delimited text file from Excel or another application, but you can't import data directly from Excel. Click the Apply button (the checkmark) when you've finished.

For your reference, add labels for a legend by entering titles across the top row in the Graph Data window. For pie charts with more than a few sections, the legend provides a helpful key. You will remove the legend later in this technique, before you convert the pie chart to 3D.

Enter labels across the top

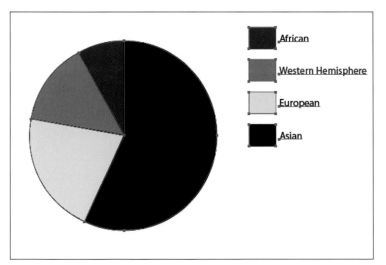

Enter the values for the pie graph

4 Deselect the graph. Using the direct selection tool, click individual wedges of the pie chart and color each with a different solid color.

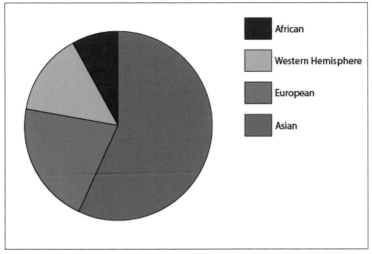

Paint the pie pieces with solid colors

3D graphing

1 Use the selection tool to select the entire pie chart. In the Color palette, stroke the pie chart with None.

You need to remove the stroke because it will change the color of the sides of the pie chart when you add the 3D effect.

2 If your pie graph does not have a legend, skip to step 4.

3 If your pie graph has a legend, first copy it and then remove it. To copy the legend in the Layers palette, drag the layer to the New Layer button at the bottom of the palette, and then click the eye icon next to the duplicate layer to hide it. To remove the legend, choose Object > Graph > Data to open the Graph Data dialog box. Shift-select the top row that contains the text labels and choose Edit > Cut to remove them. Then Shift-select the entire block of data and choose Edit > Cut. Shift-select the row above it and choose Edit > Paste. Click the Apply button (the checkmark) and close the Graph Data dialog box.

Using 3D patterns

When you extrude an object that's painted with a pattern, the extrusion color is the pattern. In the Pie Chart technique, try painting some of the slices with pattern fills for some very interesting results. (To locate a pattern, choose Window > Swatch Libraries > Other Library > Presets > Patterns.) Don't stroke the pie pieces, because the stroke also will extrude and cover up the pattern extrusion effect. The following example used line patterns with the same design but filled with different colors.

Pie chart painted with line patterns and extruded

The legend needs to be removed and the data moved up to the top row in the Graph Data dialog box to prevent the pie chart from self-intersecting or changing size when the bevel is applied.

Delete the labels and select the data   *Paste the data in the top row*

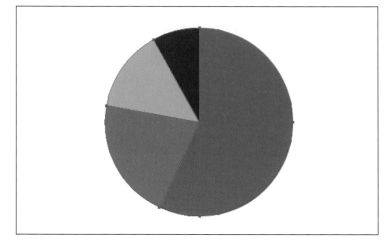

Pie chart without strokes and legend

4 If the pie chart is not already selected, use the selection tool to select the entire pie chart. Choose Effect > 3D > Extrude & Bevel. Set an Extrude Depth amount; then use the track cube to adjust how you want the chart to appear, or choose a preset view in the Position pop-up menu. Don't click OK yet.

The following example uses the Off-Axis-Bottom preset view.

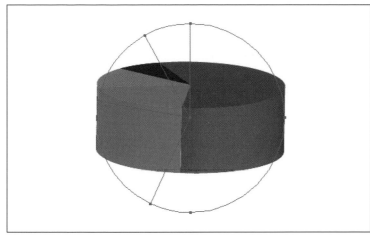

Select a view and extrude depth for the 3D pie chart

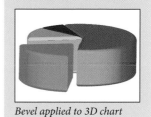
5   Click the More Options button in the 3D Extrude & Bevel Options dialog box to display the lighting controls. In the Surface section of the dialog box, click the New Light button below the preview to add a light or two if necessary, and position them so that your chart is clear and bright. You can also Option/Alt-drag a light in the preview to duplicate it. When you've finished, click OK in the dialog to apply the 3D effect. Deselect.

More so than with other 3D objects, you have to pay attention to the lighting of pie charts to prevent some of the sections from appearing dark or muddy.

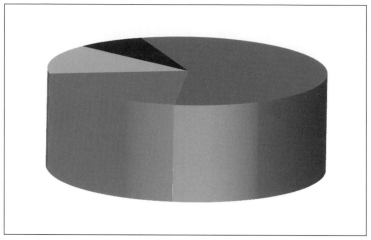

Adjust the lighting

6   Using the direct selection tool, select a pie wedge and pull
it out from the center of the pie. This creates an exploded
view of the chart.

Because the chart is grouped and the 3D appearance is a live
effect, you can still make changes to your chart.

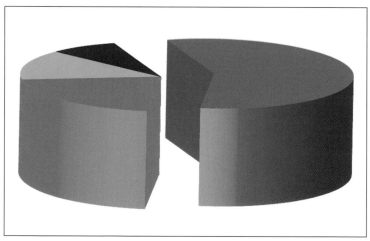

Separate a wedge from the pie chart

Variation: Transparent graph wedges

Here's how to make the wedges of your graph look transparent.

1   Use the direct selection tool to select an individual wedge. In the Transparency palette, change the Opacity value.

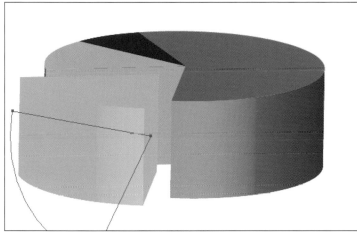

Select a wedge and change its transparency

2   To see the effect of the transparency, select the pie chart. In the Appearance palette (Window > Appearance), double-click the 3D Extrude & Bevel item to display the 3D Extrude & Bevel Options dialog box. If its lighting options aren't visible, click the More Options button. At the bottom of the dialog box, select the Draw Hidden Faces option and click OK.

Surface:	Plastic Shading	
	Light Intensity:	100%
	Ambient Light:	58%
	Highlight Intensity:	48%
	Highlight Size:	100%
	Blend Steps:	84
Shading Color:	Black	
☐ Preserve Spot Colors	☑ Draw Hidden Faces	

Select the Draw Hidden Faces option

> ### Editing in real time
>
> When you're working in the 3D Extrude & Bevel Options dialog box, you can hold down Shift while adjusting any of the sliders to see the image update in real time. This is especially helpful when adjusting the lighting.

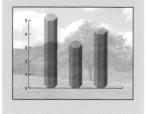
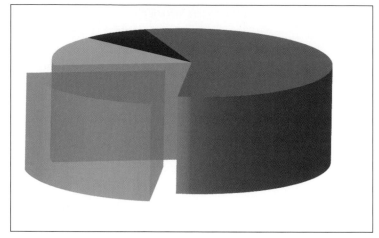

Completed transparent pie wedge

Variation: Surface-mapped labels

For another effect, you can map art to the faces of your wedges.

1 Create the symbols you want to apply to the faces of the pie chart pieces. To create a symbol, just drag the symbol artwork onto the Symbols palette. Double-click the symbol in the Symbol palette to name it. This example shows four different type objects (chart labels) made into symbols.

2 Select the pie chart you made with the 3D Graphing technique. In the Appearance palette, double-click the 3D Extrude & Bevel item to open the 3D Extrude & Bevel dialog box. Turn on the Preview option. Click the Map Art button.

3 Select a surface onto which to map the artwork, clicking the Surface arrows to cycle through the surfaces; the selected surface is highlighted in red on your pie chart. Choose a symbol from the Symbol pop-up menu, and position it to your liking in the Map Art window. You may need to rotate or scale the symbol to fit it to the face. To add shading to the symbol, select the Shade Artwork (Slower) option at the bottom of the Map Art dialog box.

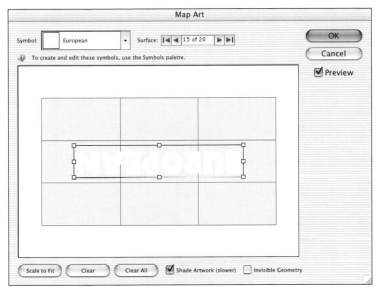

Map a symbol to one of the faces of the pie chart

4 Repeat step 3 to apply symbols to the remaining surfaces, as desired. Click OK and then click OK again to exit the 3D Extrude & Bevel dialog box.

Completed pie chart with mapped symbols

Don't ungroup the graph

A graph is a special kind of group. Ungrouping a graph should be done only if you're sure that you have finished making all changes to the graph. Once you ungroup a graph, it's no longer a graph object and is just regular shapes. In addition, if you have a 3D effect applied at the group level, deleting that group discards the 3D effect.

36 Banners with graphics

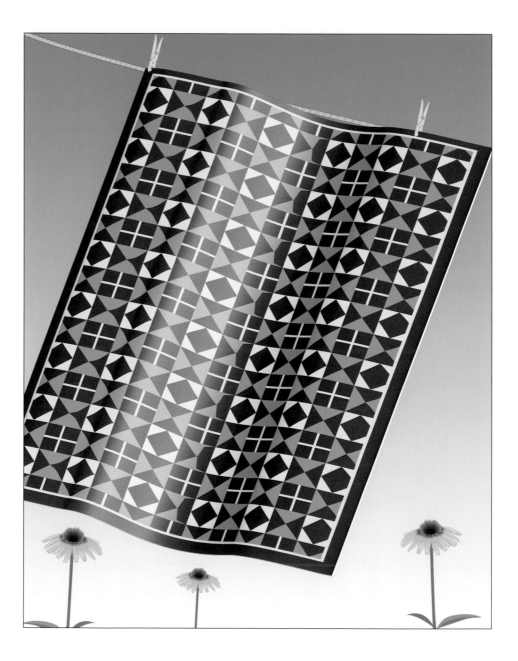

Applying a logo or artwork to a three-dimensional banner or ribbon is easy when you use the 3D Effect feature. First, you will create a logo or graphic and save it as a symbol. Then you'll make a path that represents the curved edge of the banner. You will extrude that curved edge to create a banner with the 3D Extrude effect. Once the banner is created, you can apply the artwork to the front surface of the banner with the Map Artwork feature of 3D Extrude. The nice thing about using the live 3D effect is that you can cdit it and make many changes without recreating your artwork.

Shortcut: Create a symbol

To turn the selected artwork into a symbol instance at the same time as defining it as a symbol, press Shift as you drag the artwork onto the Symbols palette.

1   Make a new layer in the Layers palette and name it Banner Art. Create the type or graphics that will appear on your banner. Paint the artwork and type.

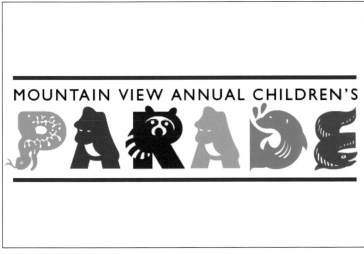

Create the banner type or graphics and paint it

2   Select the banner artwork and Option/Alt-click the New Symbol button at the bottom of the Symbols palette. In the Symbol Options dialog box, name the symbol Banner Logo and click OK to add the symbol to the Symbols palette.

To apply the banner artwork to the banner as a live 3D effect, you must first save the artwork as a symbol.

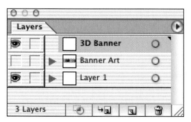

Name the new symbol   *Banner logo symbol added to the Symbols palette*

3   In the Layers palette, click the eye icon next to the Banner Art layer to hide the layer. You will not need this artwork again unless you make changes later.

4   In the Layers palette, Option/Alt-click the New Layer button. Name the new layer 3D Banner and click OK.

Create the 3D Banner layer

5   Select the pen tool in the toolbox. Draw a curve that defines the edge of your banner.

Try to keep the curve simple and without too many points. If the curve gets too complex, the artwork won't map onto it easily.

6   With the path selected, paint it with a fill of None and a stroke of whatever color you want your banner to be. In the following example, the banner will be white, so it was painted with a white stroke.

Create the path that defines the edge of the banner

7   With the curve still selected, choose Effect > 3D > Extrude
    & Bevel. Set the Position to Off-Axis Top and set the
    Extrude Depth value to an amount that will accomodate
    your banner graphic. Don't worry if you don't get the depth
    exactly right; you can go back and change it in a later step.
    Turn on the Preview option to view the extrusion.

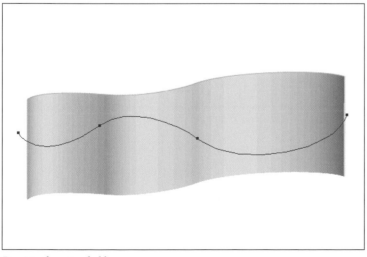

Preview the extruded banner

Creating different views

Once you've created a banner
or ribbon, you can change
the position from which it's
viewed. The mapped artwork
will still be there, but it will
change angles along with the
banner. If you adjust the position, you may have to change
the lighting. Create a custom
position or use the presets.
Here are just a few of the
preset angles you can try.

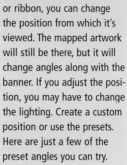

Off-Axis Top position

Isometric Left position

Isometric Right position

Off-Axis Right position

8 Click the Map Art button in the Extrude & Bevel dialog box to open the Map Art dialog box. Click the Next Surface (right arrowhead) button until the front surface is highlighted in the preview. Make sure that you pick the light gray surface, not the dark gray surface. (Dark gray indicates that the surface is hidden.)

Depending on your artwork, you may have more or fewer surfaces than the following example. If you are confused about which surface to pick, be sure to select the Preview option in the Map Art dialog box, to help you see the effect when you perform the next step.

Select the surface onto which to map the artwork

9 From the Symbol pop-up menu in the dialog box, choose the Banner Logo symbol. Move the Map Art dialog box away from the artwork so that you can see whether the symbol is mapping properly onto the correct surface.

If the symbol is not visible and the Preview option is on, you may need to choose a different surface on which to map the symbol. Set the current surface symbol to None, select a different surface number, and repeat step 9.

![Map Art dialog box showing the Banner Logo symbol mapped onto a surface with the text "MOUNTAIN VIEW ANNUAL CHILDREN'S PARADE"]

Map Art

Symbol: [Banner Logo] ▾ Surface: |◀ ◀ 6 of 6 ▶ ▶|

ⓘ To create and edit these symbols, use the Symbols palette.

OK Cancel ☑ Preview

MOUNTAIN VIEW ANNUAL CHILDREN'S
PARADE

Scale to Fit Clear Clear All ☐ Shade Artwork (slower) ☐ Invisible Geometry

Select the Banner Logo symbol to map onto the surface

10 If the artwork fits the surface width, skip to step 11. If the artwork doesn't fit the surface width, either scale it visually by Shift-dragging the corner handles, or click the Scale to Fit button. The Scale to Fit button will distort the artwork and fit it to the edges of the surface.

If the artwork is too short or tall for the surface, you can adjust the height in step 12.

11 To reposition the artwork on the surface, move the pointer to the center of the artwork. Then drag the artwork into the desired position. Click OK to exit the Map Art dialog box. Do not exit the Extrude & Bevel dialog box yet.

12 If the artwork fits the surface height, skip to step 13. If the artwork is too tall, increase the Extrude Depth value in the Extrude & Bevel dialog box; if the artwork is too short, decrease the Extrude Depth value.

Fitting symbols onto multiple surfaces

Some ribbons or banners are complex or have many curves. In those cases, the front face of the banner may be divided into more than one surface. If you encounter this situation, you can apply the same symbol to the other surface and then match them up. Here's how:

1 Follow the Banners With Graphics technique.

2 Repeat steps 9 and 10 for the second front surface.

3 In step 11, reposition the second surface so that it registers with the first surface.
4 Continue with step 12.

Calculating blend steps for 3D objects

When you use surface shading on 3D objects, you must decide how many blend steps to use. It's important to use a number that is not too small. If you use too few steps, you could end up with banding in your gradations. If you use too many, the file may be slow and very large due to the increased number of paths generated. The number of blend steps depends on the following factors:

- The size of the artwork.
- The largest percentage of change in color.
- The final destination for the artwork (screen or print).

Illustrator Help includes a chart that you can use to figure out the number of steps needed; see the topic "Calculating maximum blend length based on color change." You will have to modify the instructions a bit because they are written for blends with the blend tool, not 3D objects.

Instead of measuring the entire blend, as the Help instructions state, measure the largest blend expanse in your 3D object. For the final banner at the bottom of the facing page, the largest blend expanse measured 1.6 inches. The recommended number of steps for the next closest blend length, 1.8 inches, was 60, so that was the value used.

In the following example, because the artwork was taller than the banner, the Extrude depth was increased.

Adjust the Extrude Depth value to fit the artwork

13 To correct the lighting, click the More Options button. Adjust the lighting to your taste and artwork.

In the following example, a second light was added and the first light was moved. The Light intensity of the first light was changed to 54%. The Light intensity of the second light was changed to 41%.

Adjust the lighting

Lighting adjusted

14 If you also want the mapped artwork to be shaded, click
the Map Art button and click the Shade Artwork (Slower)
button. Click OK to exit the Extrude & Bevel dialog box.
Add any other graphics to complete the illustration.
Save the file.

Completed illustration

It's always fun hanging crepe-paper streamers at a party, but it's even more fun to draw them in Illustrator. At first glance, Illustrator doesn't have the ability to twist 3D objects. But you can take advantage of artwork mapping and a hidden feature called Invisible Geometry to get a very realistic (and easy!) streamer.

1   Begin your streamer by creating it as it would look flat. Include the text and the background.

Create the streamer art

2   Once you've created the art, define it as a symbol by selecting it and Option/Alt-clicking the New Symbol button at the bottom of the Symbols palette. Name your symbol descriptively.

Create a symbol

Positioning symbols

When you place a symbol in the Map Art dialog box, you can adjust the size, rotation, and position of your art using the bounding box.

To rotate your art, position your cursor just outside one of the corner handles. When you see the rotate cursor, drag to rotate. To reposition your artwork, move the pointer into the bounding box area; when the pointer changes to a crossed-arrow icon, you can drag the artwork. To scale the artwork, move your cursor to one of the corner points. When the cursor changes to a double-headed arrow, you can scale the artwork.

3 Draw a tall thin rectangle, and fill it with any color. Set the stroke to None.

What you're going to do now is "wrap" your streamer around a cylinder so that the streamer looks twisted, but you'll hide the cylinder so that only the streamer art is visible. For a tighter twist effect, use a narrower shape. For a looser twist, make your rectangle slightly wider.

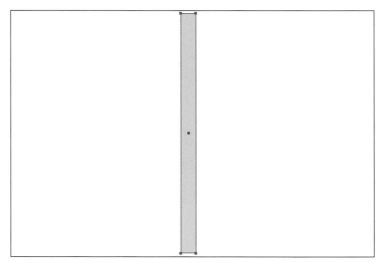

Create a tall thin rectangle

4 Select the rectangle and choose Effect > 3D > Revolve. Turn on the Preview option.

5 Click the Map Art button and turn on the Preview option. Use the Surface arrow buttons to step through the surfaces (indicated by red highlights in the artwork) until you have highlighted the side of the cylinder. From the Symbol pop-up menu, choose the symbol you created and position it at an angle that overlaps the visible and nonvisible areas.

6 At the bottom of the Map Art dialog box, select the Invisible Geometry option. This hides the cylinder, revealing only the mapped symbol. If you want the mapped symbol to be shaded, turn on the Shade Artwork option.

Map the symbol onto the revolved cylinder and use Invisible Geometry

7 Click OK to go back to the 3D Revolve Options dialog box, and use the track cube to rotate the cylinder to the desired angle. Click OK to apply the effect.

Completed crepe-paper streamer

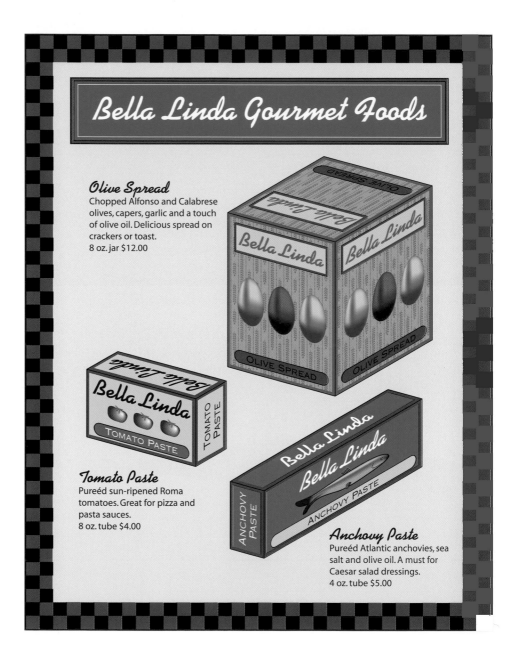

Bella Linda Gourmet Foods

Olive Spread
Chopped Alfonso and Calabrese olives, capers, garlic and a touch of olive oil. Delicious spread on crackers or toast.
8 oz. jar $12.00

Tomato Paste
Pureéd sun-ripened Roma tomatoes. Great for pizza and pasta sauces.
8 oz. tube $4.00

Anchovy Paste
Pureéd Atlantic anchovies, sea salt and olive oil. A must for Caesar salad dressings.
4 oz. tube $5.00

When it comes to package design, Illustrator is the industry standard. A traditional challenge for designers has always been finding a way to present packaging comps to clients. Illustrator's 3D features make it easy to create lifelike representations of designs and provide clear instruction to production houses and printers. This technique shows how to create a front 3D view for a six-sided box-type package.

1 Begin by creating the art for each of the individual panels of your package. Create your art at actual size; this way you can use the same file for the final art. (The artboard can be as large as 227.5-inches square; to set the artboard size, choose File > Document Setup.) For this project you should have six panels in total: one for the front, back, two sides, and top and bottom.

Create the flat art for the six panels of the package

2 Set up a border rectangle for each panel at actual size, even if the art doesn't fill the entire panel. Give this border a fill and stroke of None. Select the front panel and, using the Info palette, note the front panel's width and height. Select a side panel and note its width. You will use these values in steps 6 and 7.

Rotating the panels

Before mapping art onto a 3D package, you may need to transform the art. It's much easier to change the panel art before you make it a symbol. Follow these steps using the listed values and tools.

1 Select the panel to change.
2 Double-click the transformation tool described. Enter the amount given, and click OK.

Untransformed panels

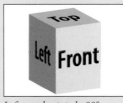

Left panel rotated –90°

Untransformed panels

Right panel rotated 90°, Back reflected vertically

Adding the invisible box will make it much easier to position the art on the 3D shape later. You also may want to group the border rectangle and each panel to make them easier to select.

3 Read "Rotating the panels" on page 279 before you create your symbols.

4 Select the front panel art and drag it into the Symbols palette to define it as a symbol. Double-click the symbol in the Symbols palette and name it Front Panel (naming the symbol descriptively will help you find it more easily).

5 Repeat step 4 for the remaining five panels, naming them Back Panel, Right Panel, Left Panel, Top Panel and Bottom Panel respectively.

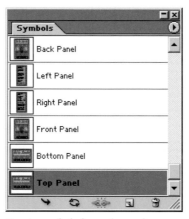

Create symbols for each panel

6 Using the rectangle tool, click once on-screen and enter the exact dimensions you noted in step 2 for the front panel of your package. Specify a fill of 15% black and a stroke of None; these values will make the shape easier to view and work with. The panels you created will cover the color anyway.

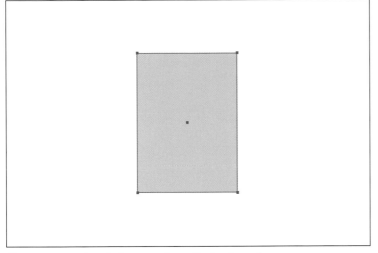

Create a gray rectangle the same size as the front panel

7   With the rectangle selected, choose Effect > 3D Extrude & Bevel and turn on the Preview option. Leave the view set to the default Off-Axis Front. In the Extrude Depth field, enter the exact width of the package's side panel, referring to your notes in step 2. Although this field is set to points, you can enter your value in inches by typing "in" after the number, and Illustrator will automatically convert the value for you.

Enter an extrude depth

8   Click the Map Art button. In the Map Art dialog box, turn on the Preview option. Position the dialog boxes so that you can see the preview art on your artboard.

9   Starting with the front panel, select the surface using the arrow buttons (the red highlight in the artwork indicates which surface is selected). Choose the Front Panel symbol for that side of your package from the Symbol pop-up menu.

If the symbol is a different size than the panel, click the Scale to Fit button. Don't click OK yet.

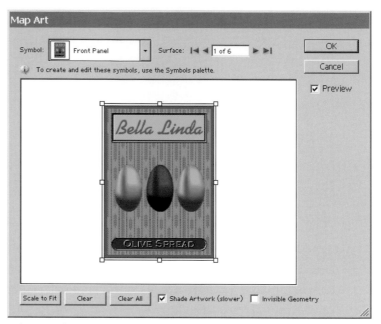

Select a surface and apply the appropriate symbol

10 Repeat step 9 to map artwork to the remaining sides, choosing the corresponding symbol from the Symbols pop-up menu.

Map a symbol to each surface

11 For a more realistic representation, select the Shade Artwork option. Depending on the artwork used on the panels, this option may significantly affect performance. When you are satisfied with the effect, click OK. Click OK in the 3D Extrude & Bevel Options dialog box.

Choose the Shade Artwork option for more realism

12 To increase the effects resolution, choose Effect > Document Raster Effects Settings. Change the resolution and click OK.

It's best to change this setting at the end of a project because it can significantly increase rendering times. Artwork that is mapped onto a 3D surface is rasterized at the Document Raster Effects Resolution setting. The default resolution is 72 ppi even if you've mapped a high-resolution image.

Notice the difference between the olives in the preceding illustration (300 pixels per inch) and the olives in the illustration after step 10 (72 pixels per inch).

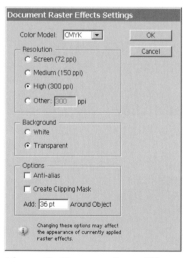

Change the Document Raster Effects settings

Multiple views

1 To create a second view of the package, Option-drag your completed 3D object to make a copy of it.

Duplicate the package

2 With the object still selected, double-click the 3D Extrude & Bevel item in the Appearance palette. Using the track cube or a preset view, change the rotation to a different view. Click OK.

3 Repeat steps 1 and 2 for as many views as you want. To learn how to add cast shadows to your illustration, see the Transparent Shadows technique on page 56.

Create multiple views of the package

Blending 3D objects

Create multiple views instantly or build an animation by blending between two 3D objects with different views. The blend rotates the intermediate objects in 3D space.

1 Create a 3D object; copy it.
2 Select the copy. Change its view by double-clicking the 3D Extrude & Bevel item in the Appearance palette, and rotating the position in the dialog box.

Create two 3D objects

3 Select both objects. Choose Object > Blend > Make.

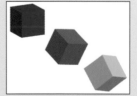

Create a blend

4 Choose Object > Blend > Blend Options. Choose Specified Steps, enter a value, and click OK.

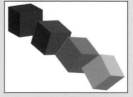

Adjust the blend steps

Using Illustrator's 3D effect to create extruded objects is nice, but the real power of Illustrator's 3D effect becomes apparent with the Revolve effect. In this technique, you'll see how Illustrator's 3D features can be used for packaging, and for illustrative purposes. A seemingly complex shape can be drawn in just a few steps, with the added benefit of being able to adjust the angle or position of the final illustration at will.

1   Begin by drawing a profile of the bottle that you want to create. This example shows each part drawn as a separate shape because the bottle parts will be colored differently: the nipple is one shape, the plastic ring is a second, and the bottle itself is a third.

To give the appearance of milk inside the bottle, a fourth shape was drawn and sent behind the shape of the bottle.

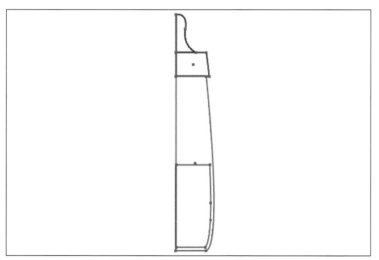

Create the profile of the bottle

2   Apply a fill color to each of the objects and set their stroke to None. In the example, the milk shape was colored white.

Visualizing the axis

When drawing a profile that will be rotated, it is helpful to create a vertical guide to use as a visual for the axis. The axis of a 3D revolve is the line around which the object revolves. The guide also makes it easier for you to align objects to the axis. To create an axis guide, do this:

1   Choose View > Show Rulers (Command/Ctrl+R).

2   Choose View > Snap to Point to turn on the Snap to Point feature. This will assist you in aligning shapes to the guide.

3   Drag a guide from the ruler by clicking the vertical ruler and dragging to the area where you want a guide. Release the mouse button to position the guide.

4   Create the profile shapes using the guide to align the objects. When you position the pen tool over the guide, the Snap to Point feature will ensure that your point is directly on top of the guide line.

Profile shapes aligned to guide

Testing the shape

It's difficult to visualize how the final outside shape will appear when only half of the outer edge of the bottle is visible. Before you revolve a profile, try this:

1 Create the profile with a guide for the axis (see "Visualizing the axis" on page 287) and select it. Don't close the shape along the axis yet.

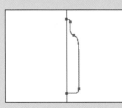

2 Select the reflect tool in the toolbox. Option/Alt-click anywhere on the axis guide line to open the Reflect dialog box. Choose Vertical and click Copy.

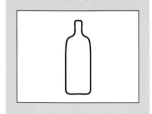

3 Evaluate the shape. Edit the path; if needed, delete the copy, and repeat step 2 until you are satisfied. Close the edge along the axis with the pen tool.

3 Select all of the shapes using the selection tool and group them (Object > Group).

Grouping the objects is a necessary step when applying a 3D effect using multiple shapes. For the object to appear correctly, you apply the 3D effect to the group.

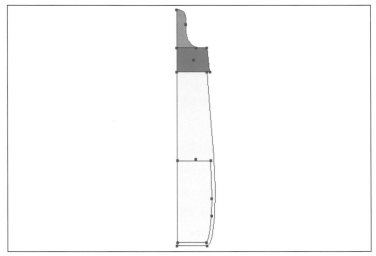

Paint the shapes with a fill but no stroke

4 Using the direct selection tool, click the bottle shape once to select just that shape (not the entire group). Choose Window > Transparency to display the Transparency palette and change the Opacity value to 50%. This lets you see the contents inside the bottle when the 3D effect is applied.

In the following example, the transparency is hard to see at this stage because the shape underneath (the milk) is white. It will show up in step 6.

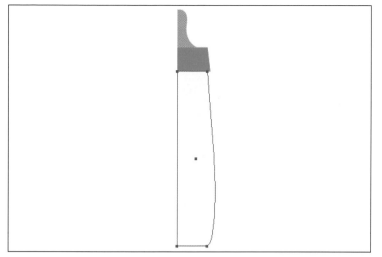

Change the opacity of the bottle

5   Select the entire group (the Group item should be selected
    in the Appearance palette) and choose Effect > 3D >
    Revolve. Turn on the Preview option. Using the track cube
    or the Position pop-up menu, rotate the bottle to the angle
    you want. Don't click OK yet.

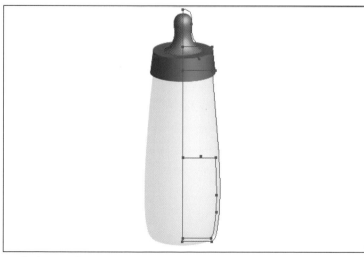

Apply the 3D effect

Right and left profiles

By default, Illustrator revolves objects from the left edge of the object. You can revolve from the right edge if you've drawn your profile from the other side. And, if you want a hollow space in the middle of your object—as in the vase here—you can add an offset value.

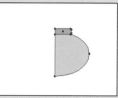

Original profile

Revolved from left edge

Revolved from right edge

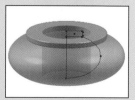

Revolved with offset

6 To make the transparency of the bottle visible, click the More Options button to show the Surface options. Select the Draw Hidden Faces option. You should now be able to see through the bottle.

Apply the Draw Hidden Faces option to make the bottle transparent

7 To brighten the dull plastic of the bottle, using the Surface options add a light or two and increase the Highlight Intensity setting.

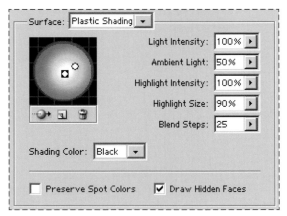

Add a new light or two to increase brightness and reflections

8 If you have artwork to apply to the bottle, click the Map Artwork button and click the Surface arrow buttons to step through the different surfaces (a red highlight in the artwork indicates the selected surface) until you reach the outside of the bottle. Apply and position your symbol and click OK. Click OK again in the 3D Revolve Options dialog box.

Completed 3D transparent bottle

Watch your (blend) steps

The default number of blend steps for a 3D object is 25, which is OK for some applications. But if you plan to print your object on a high-end press, you should increase that number to 100 or even more, depending on your object color and lighting settings. Note that a higher setting will slow performance, so it's best to change this setting right before you send the artwork to print.

25 steps

50 steps

150 steps

40 | Quick spheres

Entering precise measurements

Need to create a 3-inch circle but your measurement unit preferences are set to points? Don't change your preferences. Illustrator will convert any measurement you enter in a text box as long as you enter the unit name or abbreviation after the number. For example, if your preference unit is points but you want to create a 3-inch circle, select the circle tool and simply click it once to open the dialog box. Then enter "3 in" or "3 inches" or "3 inch" and the number will be converted to points automatically. Click OK to create your 3-inch circle. Following are more measurement terms you can use in the dialog boxes:

- inch, inches, in
- millimeters, millimetres, mm
- Qs (one Q equals .25 mm)
- centimeters, centimetres, cm
- points, p, pt
- picas, pc
- pixel, pixels, px

If you don't want to go to the trouble of using the 3D Effects to create a sphere and adjust its lighting, try using this technique. It's fast and easy because it just uses a radial gradient to create the desired effect. You won't get the sophisticated controls that you do with the 3D effects, but sometimes you just need a quick, simple sphere.

1   Select the ellipse tool, press Shift, and drag to create a circle.

2   Choose Window > Gradient or click the Gradient tab to display the Gradient palette. Create a new gradient with the highlight color on the left side of the gradient slider and the shadow color on the right. Choose Radial for the Type.

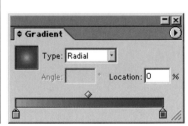

Create a circle   *Create a radial gradient*

3   Select the circle, if deselected, and fill it with the radial gradient.

By default, the highlight color (the leftmost on the Gradient Palette slider) is in the center of the circle.

4 Select the gradient tool. Drag from the point where you want the highlight, to the point where you want the shadow to begin.

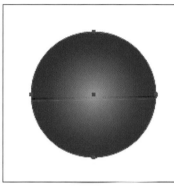

Fill the circle with the gradient

Reposition the highlight

5 In the Gradient palette, drag the diamond above the gradient slider to increase or decrease the amount of highlight in the sphere then deselect.

In this example, the diamond was moved from the 50% position to the 60% position to increase the size of the highlight.

Change the size of the highlight

Adding colors to gradients with the eyedropper tool

Want to add a color to your gradient from another shape or placed object within the file? Use the eyedropper tool. Select the gradient-filled object. Display the Gradient palette by choosing Window > Gradient. Click the gradient stop that you want to change. Select the eyedropper tool in the toolbox. Hold down Shift and click the color you want to add to the gradient. You can click any object—another gradient, a raster image, or a gradient mesh object, for example. You won't get predictable results by clicking objects filled with patterns or that use live effects, however.

Traditionally, drawing a shape with a realistic 3D appearance required the knowledge of vanishing points, lighting, and geometry, along with a double dose of patience. Using Illustrator's 3D effects can make these tasks a lot easier once you understand their capabilities. Drawing wires is a good example of how you can create something seemingly complicated with just a few clicks of the mouse.

Curved wires

To create curved wires, you can use a bevel effect to get the appearance of a round wire. If the paths don't overlap each other, you can apply the 3D Bevel effect to all of them at once. If they do overlap each other, you will need to apply the effect to each path individually.

1 Draw several curved paths. Set the stroke width to 4 points and apply a stroke color. (You may have to reapply the stroke color in step 7). All of the paths should have a fill of None.

2 Select one of the paths.

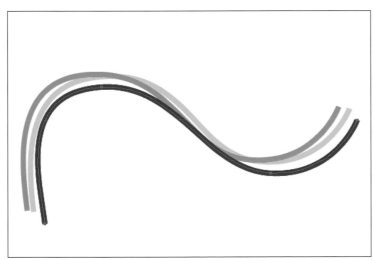

Create the paths and select one of them

Creating your own bevels

You can create your own custom bevel designs. To do this, you must open a special file in the Adobe Illustrator CS folder. With Illustrator running, choose Open and navigate to Adobe Illustrator CS > Plug-ins > Bevels.ai. Click Open. When the file opens, follow the instructions for creating and saving custom bevels in the Bevels.ai file.

3 With the path selected, choose Effect > 3D > Extrude & Bevel. Turn on the Preview option. Set the Extrude Depth amount to something small, like 5 points.

4 From the Bevel pop-up menu, choose the Rounded option. Then set the Bevel Height to 2 points and choose the Bevel Extent In option. Click OK. If a warning box appears, click OK.

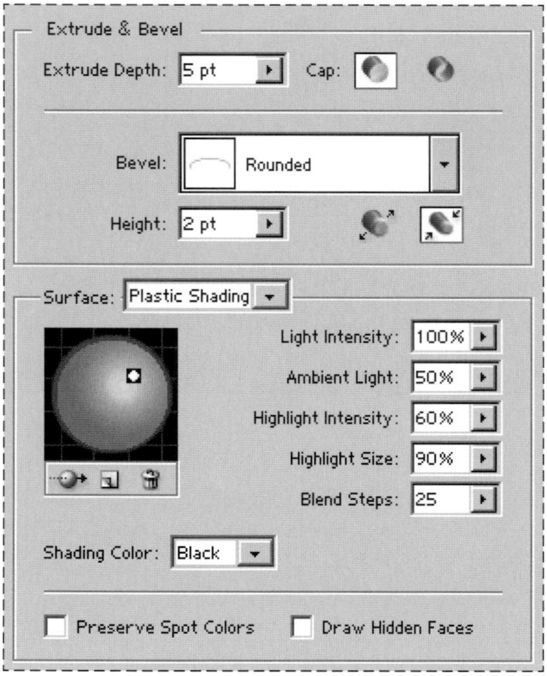

Apply a small round bevel

5 Now save the appearance of this wire as a graphic style to use on the other paths. With the path still selected in the Appearance palette, Option/Alt-click the New Style button at the bottom of the Graphic Styles palette. Name the style 5-pt wire.

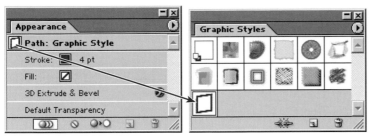

Drag the thumbnail from the Appearance palette to the Graphic Styles palette

6   Select one of the other paths. Click the 5 pt-Wire style in the Graphic Styles palette to apply the 3D effect. The color changes to the color of the first path. You will change that in the next step.

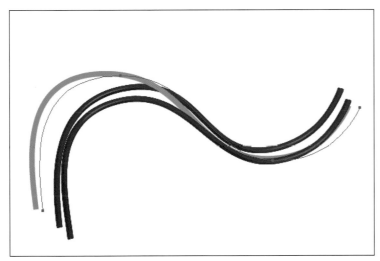

Apply the 5 pt-wire style to another path

7   With the path still selected, change the stroke color, if desired. If you want to, repeat step 5 to save this newly colored 5-pt Wire as a different style.

8   Repeat steps 6 and 7 for any other paths that you want to be 3D wires.

Creating a paper clip

You can use the Curved Wires technique to create curved wire for other shapes, such as a paper clip. Start with a path in the coiled shape of a paper clip, and finish it by applying a soft drop shadow for effect.

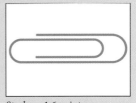

Stroke = 1.6 points, 40% black

Extruded stroke with drop shadow added

Making different wire thicknesses

The wire thickness in the Curved Wire technique is 4 points. To vary the wire thickness, see these illustrations for some different values.

Stroke = 4 points,
Extrude Depth = 5 points,
Extrude Height = points

Stroke = 6 points,
Extrude Depth = 7 points,
Extrude Height = 3 points

Stroke = 10 points,
Extrude Depth = 12 points,
Extrude Height = 5 points

Stroke = 20 points,
Extrude Depth = 20 points,
Extrude Height = 10 points

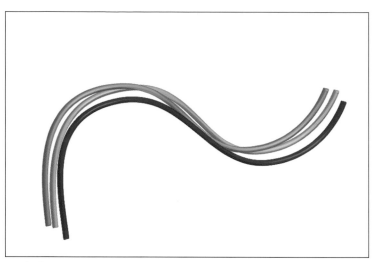

Apply the 5 pt-Wire style to other paths and change their stroke color

Straight coaxial cable

1   Draw three rectangles (as shown in the following illustration), each one a bit longer than the other, with the following width and fill values and a stroke of None: Left rectangle: 1.5-points wide, 40% Black fill; Middle rectangle: 16-points wide, White fill; Right rectangle: 6-points wide, 80% Black fill.

If you want your cable to be thicker or thinner, use the values listed above and then scale the path later.

2   Using the Align palette (Window > Align), align the bottom edge of the rectangles so that the corners touch. Make sure that the edges and corners align as shown in the following illustration.

3   Select all three shapes and group them. This lets you apply the 3D effect to all of the shapes as one and ensures that they are revolved together instead of individually in step 4.

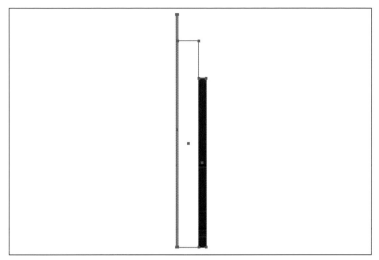

Create three rectangles and group them

4 Select the group and choose Effect > 3D > Revolve. Turn on
the Preview option. To give the gray plastic a bit more life,
click More Options; in the Surface section, add a second
light, increase the Highlight Intensity to 100%, and set the
Highlight Size to 75%.

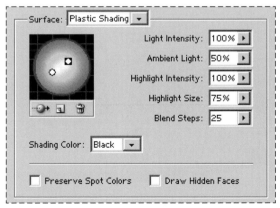

Add a second light

5 When you are satisfied with the preview, click OK.

Revolved rectangles

6 To give the cable mesh shielding, draw a mesh design and Option/Alt-drag it onto the Symbols palette to save it as a symbol. You will use this in step 7.

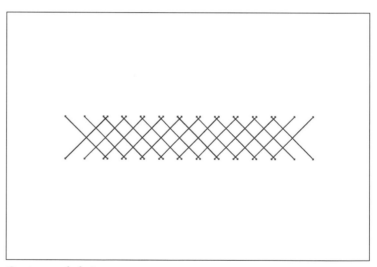

Create a mesh design

7 Select the wire group and double-click the 3D Revolve effect in the Appearance palette to edit the effect. Click the Map Art button and click the Surface arrow buttons to step through the surfaces until you highlight the white center part of the cable. (The red highlight in the artwork indicates the selected surface.) From the Symbol pop-up menu, choose the mesh symbol you created in step 6. Click the Scale to Fit button, adjust the size if necessary, and click OK. Click OK again to exit the 3D Revolve Options dialog box.

This technique only works on straight vertical paths because the wire is created by revolving around a vertical axis. Trying this with a path drawn on an angle will result in a cone shape. However, once you've created the 3D wire, you can rotate it to any angle in 3D space in the 3D Revolve Options dialog box. Simply select the artwork, double-click the effect in the Appearance palette, and use the track cube in the 3D Revolve Options dialog box to rotate the view.

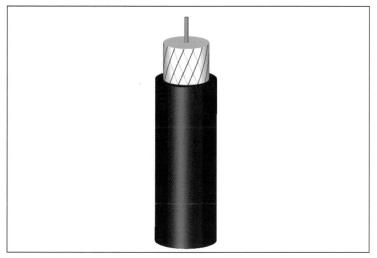

Completed coaxial cable illustration

42 | Flat graphics on curved images

Designers frequently have to apply logos, labels, logotypes, or other graphics to photographic images of products, bottles, clothing, and so on. You can add flat graphics to curved shapes in either Photoshop or Illustrator, but Illustrator offers designers more flexibility. Using this technique, you create guides for either cylindrical or spherical forms. You use these guides to design an envelope shape that will custom-fit the form to which you are applying the graphic. You then apply the graphic to the envelope. Having the graphic or type in an envelope means you can change it at any time.

1 Open a new Illustrator file, create a new layer in the Layers palette, and name it Graphic. Create the logo or graphic to be applied to a curved surface.

Create the logo on the Graphic layer

2 Option/Alt-click the New Layer button in the Layers palette to create a new layer. Name it 3D Image, and click OK. Move it beneath the Graphic layer.

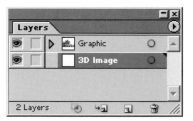

Create the 3D Image layer

3 With the 3D Image layer still selected, choose File > Place and navigate to the image file to which you will add the graphic.

You'll need to add some guides to the image next. For spherical shapes, follow the directions in the Spherical Guides technique. For cylindrical shapes, follow the directions in the Cylindrical Guides technique.

Place the image file on the 3D Image layer

Spherical guides

1 Hide the Graphic layer in the Layers palette. Move to a different area of the artboard. Select the rectangle tool in the toolbox. Create a square by Shift-dragging. The size of the square doesn't matter.

2 Divide the selected square into a grid by choosing Object > Path > Split Into Grid. Enter 6 for the number of both Rows and Columns. Enter 0 as the Gutter amount. Click OK.

Apply Split Into Grid filter to square

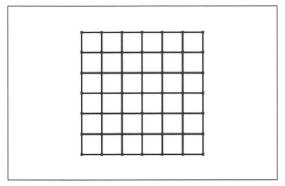

Square split into 36 separate squares

Shortcut: Move the circle while you draw

While drawing a circle or ellipse, press the spacebar to move the circle around. Don't release the mouse button or Shift key. Release the spacebar to resume drawing and then release Shift and the mouse button to finish the circle.

3   Select the ellipse tool in the toolbox, and draw a circle close to the same size as the circular object in the image and on top of that object. As you draw, press Shift to constrain the ellipse to a circle and press Option/Alt to draw from the center point.

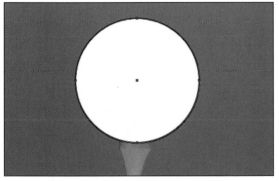

Draw a circle to match the circular object in the image

4   Use the selection tool to select both the circle and the grid you completed in steps 1 through 3.

It's important that the circle be created after the grid because the circle needs to be the frontmost object in the next step. (Alternatively, select the circle and choose Object > Arrange > Bring to Front.)

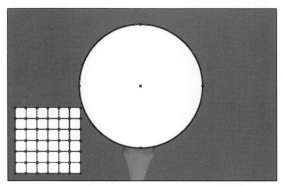

Select the grid and the circle

5 Choose Object > Envelope Distort > Make with Top Object.

Apply Envelope Distort to the selection

6 Choose Object > Envelope Distort > Expand.

You need to expand the envelope to be able to make guides in the next step.

7 With the sphere lines still selected, choose View > Guides > Make Guides. Now that you have guides, you are ready to finish the graphic distortion technique. Skip to the Curved Envelope technique.

Turn the sphere lines into guides

Cylindrical guides

1   Hide the Graphic layer in the Layers palette. Select the
    pen tool in the toolbox. Find the curve at the top of the
    cylindrical object, and draw a path that imitates it.

Draw the top curve of the cylinder

2   Deselect the path, and draw a second curve at the bottom of
    the object. With the selection tool, Shift-select both paths.

Adjusting the blend spine

When you blend two straight lines, the blend's spine is a straight line. In some cases, the spine should be curved. The following example shows the blended vertical sides adjusted to follow the curve of the horizontal guide lines. Here is how to adjust the spine curve.

1 Draw a curved line that stretches across the center of the blend. Try to match the curve of the horizontal guide lines.

2 Select the blend and the curved line.

3 Choose Object > Blend > Replace Spine.

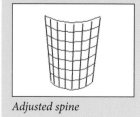

Adjusted spine

Draw the bottom curve of the cylinder

3 Choose Object > Blend > Make. Then choose Object > Blend > Blend Options. Turn on the Preview option and choose Specified Steps for the Spacing. Try different amounts until you are satisfied with the spacing. You'll need these lines to make a top and bottom guide for the graphic that you will apply to the cylinder.

4 Choose Object > Blend > Expand to convert the blend into lines.

Create a blend and then expand it

5   With the lines still selected, choose View > Guides > Make Guides.

6   Use the pen tool to create two lines that directly overlap the left and right edges of the cylindrical object. Select them both.

Draw the side edges of the cylinder

7   Repeat steps 3 through 5 of this technique to create the vertical guides for the cylinder. Continue with the Curved Envelope technique.

Create the vertical guides

Changing the guide's appearance

Depending on your artwork, it can sometimes be easier to draw shapes if you change the appearance of your guides. To do this, press Command/Ctrl+K to open the Preferences dialog box. Choose Guides & Grid from the pop-up menu. For the Guides Style, choose Dots and click OK.

Line guide style

Dots guide style

Curved envelope

1   Select the pen tool in the toolbox. Use the guidelines you created to draw a shape that will contain the graphic or logotype. Make the shape about the size you want the graphic to be.

Create the envelope shape

2   In the Layers palette, show the Graphic layer. The envelope shape should still be selected. Drag its selection indicator from the 3D Image layer up onto the Graphic layer.

The envelope shape should be in front of the graphic.

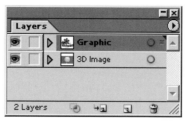

Drag the selection indicator to the Graphic layer

3   Select the envelope shape and the graphic. Don't worry if the graphic isn't the same size as the envelope. Illustrator will fix that in the next step.

4   Choose Object > Envelope Distort > Make with Top Object.

Create the envelope distortion

5 Use the direct selection tool to adjust the envelope, if necessary. Select the envelope, and choose a blending mode in the Transparency palette. This lets the shadows and texture of the photograph show through and makes the graphic look as if it is really printed on the object. The Multiply mode was used in this example.

Change the blend mode   *Completed curved logo*

A | Appendix A: Shortcuts

Frequently used shortcuts		
Shortcut	Mac OS X keystrokes	Windows keystrokes
Moving and selecting objects		
Leave a copy of a selection behind	Option+selection tool	Alt+selection tool
Constrain movement to 45° or angles set in preferences	Shift	Shift
Move selection by 1 increment (set in preferences)	Any arrow key	Any arrow key
Switch to last-used selection tool	Command	Ctrl
Switch between selection tool and direct selection/group selection tool (last used)	Command+Tab	Ctrl+Tab
Switch between direct selection tool and group selection tool	Option	Alt
Add to a selection with selection tools	Shift-click	Shift-click
Subtract a selection with selection tools	Shift-click	Shift-click
Transforming objects		
Repeat the last transformation	Command+D	Ctrl+D
Set origin point and open transform dialog box when using rotate, scale, reflect, or shear tool	Option-click	Alt-click
Duplicate and transform selection when using selection, scale, reflect, or shear tool	Option-drag	Alt-drag
Transform pattern (independent of object) when using selection, scale, reflect, or shear tool	~(tilde)-drag	~(tilde)-drag
Speeding up painting		
Return to default colors	D key	D key
Toggle between stroke and fill	X key	X key

This book assumes that before you try the techniques, you have a basic knowledge of the software and its tools, commands, and palettes. But because you are busy and can't always remember all the commands and shortcuts, this appendix contains most of the shortcuts that you'll need to use this book's techniques most efficiently. Refer to Illustrator Help for a complete list of all the keyboard shortcuts.

Frequently used shortcuts

Shortcut	Mac OS X keystrokes	Windows keystrokes
Swap fill and stroke	Shift+X	Shift+X
Select the complement for the current color fill/stroke	Command-click color bar	Ctrl-click color bar
Change the nonactive fill/stroke	Option-click color bar	Alt-click color bar
Select the inverse for the current fill/stroke	Command+Shift-click color bar	Ctrl+Shift-click color bar
Switch between paint bucket tool and eyedropper tool	Option	Alt
Sample color from an image or any color from gradient	Shift-click witrh eyedropper tool	Shift-click with eyedropper tool
Paint with straight line (any brush)	Click-Shift-click	Click-Shift-click
Show/hide Brushes palette	F5	F5
Show/hide Color palette	F6	F6
Revert	F12	F12
Change the color mode	Shift-click color bar	Shift-click color bar
Move color sliders in tandem	Shift-drag color slider	Shift-drag color slider
Switch between percentage and 0 to 255 values for RGB	Double-click to right of a numerical field	Double-click to right of a numerical field
Path editing		
Switch pen tool to convert anchor point tool	Option	Alt
Switch between add anchor point tool and delete anchor point tool	Option	Alt
Switch scissors tool to add anchor point tool	Option	Alt
Switch pencil tool to smooth tool	Option	Alt

Frequently used shortcuts for the Layers palette

Shortcut	Mac OS X keystrokes	Windows keystrokes
Cut a straight line with knife tool	Option-drag	Alt-drag
Cut at 45° or 90° with knife tool	Shift+Option-drag	Shift+Alt-drag
Viewing images		
Toggle between screen modes	F	F
Fit image in window	Double-click hand tool	Double-click hand tool
Magnify 100%	Double-click zoom tool	Double-click zoom tool
Switch to hand tool	Spacebar	Spacebar
Switch to zoom in tool	Command+spacebar	Control+spacebar
Switch to zoom out tool	Option+spacebar	Alt+spacebar
Zoom in on specified area	Drag with zoom tool	Drag with zoom tool
Release guide	Command+Shift–double-click guide	Ctrl+Shift–double-click guide
Using layers		
Create and name new layer	Option-click New Layer button	Alt-click New Layer button
Rename layer	Double-click the layer name	Double-click the layer name
Duplicate a layer	Drag layer onto New Layer button	Drag layer onto New Layer button
Duplicate and name new layer	Option-drag layer onto New Layer button	Alt-drag layer onto New Layer button
Select all objects on the layer	Option-click layer name	Alt-click layer name
Show/hide all layers but the selected one	Option-click eye icon	Alt-click eye icon
Select Outline/Preview view for the selected layer	Command-click eye icon	Ctrl-click eye icon
Expand all sublayers to display entire hierarchy	Option-click expansion triangle	Alt-click expansion triangle
Copy a selection to a new layer, sublayer, or group	Option-drag selection	Alt-drag selection
Grouping and joining		
Group selected objects	Command+G	Ctrl+G
Ungroup selected group	Shift+Command+G	Shift+Ctrl+G
Join two selected endpoints	Command+J	Ctrl+J

Frequently used shortcuts for the Layers palette

Shortcut	Mac OS X keystrokes	Windows keystrokes
Adjusting type		
Align paragraph left, right, or center	Command+Shift+L, R, or C	Ctrl+Shift+L, R, or C
Justify paragraph	Command+Shift+J	Ctrl+Shift+J
Insert soft return	Shift+Return	Shift+Enter
Increase or decrease point size	Command+Shift+ > or <	Ctrl+Shift+ > or <
Increase or decrease leading	Option+Up or Down Arrow	Alt+Up or Down Arrow
Add or remove space between two characters	Option+Right or Left Arrow	Alt+Right or Left Arrow
Add or remove space between characters by five times the increment value	Command+Option+Right or Left Arrow	Ctrl+Alt+Right or Left Arrow
Increase or decrease kerning between selected words	Option+Command+ \ or Delete	Alt+Ctrl+ \ or Backspace
Increase or decrease kerning between words by five times the increment value	Shift+Option+Command+ \ or Delete	Shift+Alt+Ctrl+ \ or Backspace
Increase or decrease baseline shift	Option+Shift+Up or Down Arrow	Alt+Shift+Up or Down Arrow

Tool shortcut keys

Start using these keyboard shortcuts to access the tools in the toolbox and you'll save yourself lots of time.

Tool	Shortcut key	Tool	Shortcut key
Selection tool	V	Reflect tool	O
Direct selection tool	A	Scale tool	S
Magic wand tool	Y	Warp tool	Shift+R
Lasso tool	Q	Free transform tool	E
Pen tool	P	Symbol sprayer tool	Shift+S
Add anchor point tool	+ (plus)	Column graph tool	J
Delete anchor point tool	- (minus)	Mesh tool	U
Convert anchor point tool	Shift+C	Gradient tool	G
Type tool	T	Eyedropper tool	I
Line segment tool	\ (backslash)	Paint bucket tool	K
Rectangle tool	M	Blend tool	W
Ellipse tool	L	Slice tool	Shift+K
Paintbrush tool	B	Scissors tool	C
Pencil too	N	Hand tool	H
Rotate tool	R	Zoom tool	Z

B | Appendix B: Combining Illustrator and Photoshop files

Avoiding color shift problems

Here's a way to avoid color shift problems when you know you'll be using an Illustrator file in Photoshop: Create the file using RGB colors. If necessary, you can convert the colors to RGB by choosing File > Document Color Mode > RGB Color.

When you're sharing artwork between the two programs, an important consideration is that Photoshop is raster-based and Illustrator is vector-based. Raster-based means that objects are described as pixels on a raster, or grid. Photoshop is better for working with organic shapes, such as those in photographs or paintings. Vector-based means that objects are mathematically described as points connected by straight or curved lines. Vector-based graphics generated in Illustrator have crisp, clear lines when scaled to any size. Because both programs can handle raster- and vector-based images, here are some things to think about when you use these programs together.

Raster versus vector

Before using Illustrator graphics in Photoshop, evaluate the artwork. Decide whether you want your shapes and type to have sharp, clean edges like the illustration below. If so, you will want to use the Copy and Paste method on page 321. When you paste the graphic, be sure to paste it as a path or shape layer to avoid rasterizing it. Then, before you print the graphic, see "Printing vector graphics from Photoshop" on page 319.

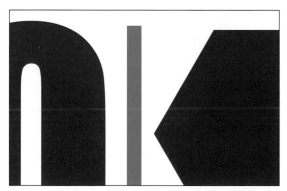

Vector artwork created in Illustrator

When you open an Illustrator file directly in Photoshop, you'll get the Rasterize dialog box. Minimize stair-stepping on curves by selecting the Anti-aliased option. Change the color mode, if desired. Note that Photoshop will rasterize the entire Illustrator file into one image layer if you open it directly. To retain the file's layers, export the file from Illustrator (see "Export method" on page 319).

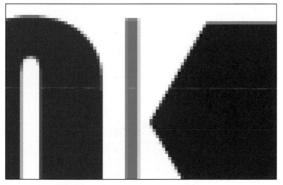

Photoshop's Rasterize dialog box

Depending on the file resolution, anti-aliasing can make the edges of objects appear fuzzy. Fuzziness with anti-aliasing is generally preferable to the stair-stepping appearance that occurs without it. Note in the illustration below that anti-aliasing does not improve the thick green line.

Anti-aliased edges after rasterization

On the other hand, if your artwork consists of vertical and horizontal lines and no curves, you can achieve better results without anti-aliasing. In this example, the green line looks

Opening multipage PDF documents

Illustrator's native format is PDF (Portable Document Format). PDF documents can contain multiple pages. Illustrator cannot save a multipage document, but many other programs can export multipage PDF files. If you try to open one of these files with Photoshop, the PDF Page Selector dialog box will appear. Just click the page thumbnail you want, and only that page will open in Photoshop. The file will be flattened and may contain transparency because Photoshop will rasterize only objects on the page, not the white page itself.

sharp, but the curves and angles in the other shapes now have a jagged edge.

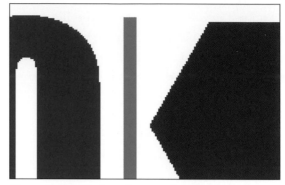

Non-anti-aliased edges after rasterization

Bringing Illustrator files into Photoshop

In Photoshop, you can choose from four ways to bring in Illustrator files: the Place command, export and open, copy and paste, or the Open command. If you want to be able to edit layers and text once the Illustrator file is opened in Photoshop, use the Export method to output the file from Illustrator. If you want to scale or transform the image to fit with an existing Photoshop file, use the Place method in Photoshop. The Copy and Paste method is best if you want to retain the outlines and use them as paths or shape layers in Photoshop.

Place method

1   In Photoshop, choose File > Place. Navigate to the Illustrator file you want to place, and click Place. Shift-drag the highlighted corners of the box to scale the image proportionally.

The advantage to this method is that you can easily transform the graphic before it is rasterized.

Placing an Illustrator graphic into a Photoshop file

2   When you have finished moving and transforming the
graphic, press Return/Enter to complete the rasterization.

Another advantage to placing a graphic is that it is placed on its
own layer with a transparent background.

Placed graphic with transparent background

Export method

1   In Illustrator, choose File > Export and select the Photoshop
(PSD) format. Be sure to name the file differently than
its Illustrator name. Click Export to open the Photoshop
Options dialog box.

2   Select the resolution for the Photoshop file. If you want to
keep the layers, select the Write Layers option. For smooth-
edged graphics, select the Anti-alias option. If your file has

Switching color modes when exporting

If you are exporting an Illustrator file to Photoshop (PSD) format, be sure to check the document color mode before you export. If you export a document that currently is in CMYK mode, you can export it as an RGB file, but you won't be able to select the Write Layers option. You can solve this problem by changing modes before you export. In Illustrator, choose File > Document Color Mode and choose the mode you want to export to. Then choose File > Export to export the Illustrator file to a PSD file. When the Photoshop Export Options dialog box opens, the Write Layers option will be available as long as the Color Model setting you choose in the Photoshop Export Options dialog box matches the color mode of the Illustrator file.

text that you want to be able to edit in Photoshop, select the Editable Text option. Click OK.

Being able to edit text is one of the advantages of using this method.

Illustrator's Export dialog box

3   Open the file in Photoshop.

The disadvantage to this method is that the file will be exactly the size of the graphics and no larger. If you want to add space around the edges of the graphic, choose Image > Canvas Size and increase the size of the canvas.

Layered Illustrator file opened in Photoshop

Copy and Paste method

1 Before copying the Illustrator graphic, choose Illustrator > Preferences > File Handling & Clipboard (Mac OS X) or Edit > Preferences > File Handling & Clipboard (Windows). To retain the paths in the file, select the AICB and Preserve Paths options. Click OK. Choose Edit > Copy to copy the selected artwork.

2 In Photoshop, choose Edit > Paste, and choose a Paste option:

- Pixels to fill the graphic with the color specified in Illustrator; to transform it before rasterizing, press Return/Enter.

- Path to paste the copy as a path in the Paths palette.

- Shape Layer to fill the graphic with the current foreground color. If you chose Shape Layer, as in the following example, the size is the exact size it was in Illustrator; to change it, choose Edit > Free Transform.

Set the Illustrator clipboard preferences

Choose a paste option

3 Click OK to paste the graphic.

Illustrator graphic is pasted as a shape at its original size

Open method

Choose File > Open and open the Illustrator file. Choose the size, mode, and resolution, and click OK.

The file will open with all layers merged onto one layer. Be sure to rename the file when saving to avoid overwriting the original Illustrator file.

Bringing Photoshop files into Illustrator

There are four different ways to bring Photoshop files into Illustrator: the Place command, drag-and-drop, copy and paste, or the Open command. The drag-and-drop or copy and paste methods are less desirable because they convert the image to a 72-ppi, RGB image. However, you can copy paths created in Photoshop and paste them into an Illustrator file with no loss of image quality. Pasted paths, however, will always be filled and stroked with None. If you open or place a layered Photoshop file, Illustrator can retain some of the layers—a nice feature if you want to be able to edit them in Illustrator.

Place command

In Illustrator, choose File > Place and turn on the Link option if you want to link the file; turn off the option if you want to embed the file.

The advantages to linking are that the file size stays small and you can update the image using the Links palette. The disadvantage is that you can't select or edit individual elements of the placed artwork.

Open command

In Illustrator, choose File > Open and select the Photoshop image. Illustrator creates an embedded image. Unfortunately, embedded images become part of the Illustrator file and increase its file size. The advantage to embedding is the ability to edit if you place a layered Photoshop file. You cannot edit a layered Photoshop file if it is linked.

Opening and placing layered Photoshop files

Choose File > Open or Place, and select a layered Photoshop file. If placing, deselect the Link option, and click Place. If opening, click Open to display the Photoshop Import Options dialog box. Choose whether to retain the layers:

- Select the Convert Photoshop Layers to Objects and Make Text Editable Where Possible option to maintain as many layers as possible. Illustrator will rasterize layers that contain layer effects, adjustment layers, certain layer modes, and clipping groups.

Select the Convert option to retain as many layers as possible

- Select the Flatten Photoshop Layers to a Single Image and Preserve Text Appearance option to flatten the file to a single layer.

Is the file linked or embedded?

The way to tell if you have linked or embedded artwork in your Illustrator file is to look at the Links palette. Linked files have no icon next to the file name. An embedded file will have a small square icon to the right of its name in the Links palette.

Linked file

Embedded file

Index

Credits

Author:	Luanne Seymour Cohen
Contributing Writer:	Mordy Golding
Book Design/Production:	Jan Martí
Production Coordinator:	Lisa Brazieal
Production Assistance:	Leslie Cutler
Cover Design:	Aren Howell
Executive Editor:	Becky Morgan
Copy Editor:	Judy Walthers von Alten
Indexer:	Judy Walthers von Alten
Technical Editor:	Barb Obermeier

Photo and illustration credits

All photography and illustration were done by Luanne Seymour Cohen unless noted in the chart below. Italics indicate large sample illustrations.

Photographer/Artist	Page number(s)
Sandy Alves	*98*
Kaoru Hollin	*104, 120*
Adobe Illustrator Clip Art, Symbols, Brushes	*8, 112, 176, 182, 266, 274*

Colophon

This book was designed and produced using Adobe InDesign CS, Adobe Photoshop CS, and Adobe Illustrator CS. The Adobe Minion Pro and Myriad Pro typefaces are used throughout the book.

Advance to the Next Level in Photoshop!

This gorgeous, full-color book from former Adobe Systems Creative Director Luanne Seymour Cohen will move you into the Studio and put your creative skills to use.

You'll learn how to:

- Create impressive painterly images
- Produce various type effects, including embossed, corroded, and metallic type
- Make realistic 3D graphics
- "Hand-color" black-and-white images
- Simulate textures from stone to wood grain to marble

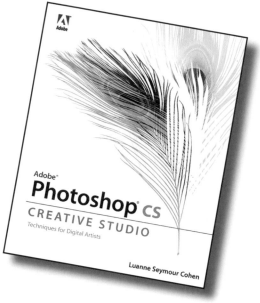

Adobe Photoshop CS Creative Studio **will move you from the Classroom to the Studio...**

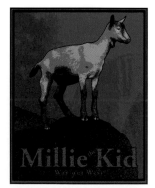